THE BOOK OF
ITALIAN COOKING

THE BOOK OF
ITALIAN COOKING

CRESCENT BOOKS
New York/Avenel, New Jersey

Recipes and photographs on the following pages
are the copyright of Merehurst Press, and credited
as follows: 16, 18, 19, 20, 21, 22, 26, 52, 53, 54, 55, 56, 57, 58,
59, 60, 61, 62, 63, 64, 65, 66, 69, 70, 72, 74, 77, 82, 83, 84, 85,
86, 87, 88, 90, 91

ISBN 0 517 10322 2

This 1993 edition published by Crescent Books, distributed by
Outlet Book Company, Inc., a Random House Company,
40 Engelhard Avenue, Avenel, New Jersey 07001

Random House
New York . Toronto . London . Sydney . Auckland

CREDITS

Contributing authors: June Budgen, Sarah Bush,
Kerenza Harries, Jacqui Hurst, Lesley Mackley, Janice Murfitt,
Cecilia Norman, Mary Norwak, Jackie Passmore, Lorna Rhodes,
Lyn Rutherford, Louise Steele, Sally Taylor, Carol Timperley,
Mary Trewby and Steven Wheeler

Photographers: Sue Atkinson, Per Ericson, David Gill,
Paul Grater, Jacqui Hurst, David Johnson, Sue Jorgensen,
Alan Newnham, Jon Stewart, Graham Tann and Philip Wymant

Typeset by: Maron Graphics Ltd., Wembley

Colour separation by: Contemporary Lithoplates Ltd.,
Fotographics Ltd., J. Film Process Ltd., Kentscan Ltd.,
Magnum Graphics Ltd., and Scantrans Pte. Ltd.

Printed in Italy

CONTENTS

INTRODUCTION

Italian food can be as simple and fresh as a Tomato & Mozzarella Salad, as hearty and robust as a warming bean and pasta soup, as light and delicate as a frothy Zabaglione, or alternatively, as indulgent as a wedge of Campari Cheesecake. Discover the color and taste of Italy, with this enticing collection of recipes.

Using modern techniques, these dishes follow the rich, long-standing Italian tradition of blending fresh ingredients simply and creatively to encourage their natural flavors. Well-known favorites are included, such as Pizza and Minestrone Soup, along with more contemporary ideas, such as Pasta Pesto Salad, Lamb & Walnut Bites and Champagne & Mint Granita. There is plenty of inspiration for entertaining with easy elegance, or putting together a hasty snack or light supper, all with that special Italian touch.

Italian cooking has been influenced by Greek, Roman and Byzantine food, together with a touch of the Orient. Drawing from natural supplies of creamy cheeses, plump olives, a vibrant wealth of fruits and vegetables, nuts, inter-estingly-shaped pastas and bountiful seafoods, the different regions of Italy have all developed their own specialties. Each area has a mixture of both rustic and refined cuisine, adapted to suit the availability of local produce. Tuscany, for example, with its gentle rolling hills and lush countryside, boasts an endless variety of bean recipes, nourishing soups and simple vegetable dishes, as well as more sophisticated recipes for asparagus and herbs. Whereas, Sicily, which lies off the Southern tip of the mainland, surrounded by sandy beaches, displays its wide range of colorful produce in pasta mixed with seafood, pizzas with olives and anchovies, and ice creams and pastries with brightly-glazed candied fruits.

Following the continuing trend for healthy eating, Italian meals consist of fairly small amounts of meat and fish, but plenty of fresh fruits and vege-tables, rice and pasta instead of fried potatoes. Olive oil replaces animal fats for cooking. An additional advantage is that most of the dishes can be quickly prepared. However, when you have more time available to spend in the kitchen,

there are step-by-step instructions for making your own pasta and pizza dough, ready for adding a lively sauce or topping. Each recipe stands on its own, or it can be mixed and matched with others to create a special occasion Italian menu of contrasting flavors, colors and textures. For example, begin with an appetizer, such as Crispy Pesto Prawns, then move on to a main course, such as Turkey Tetrazzini, accompanied by a simply-tossed green salad. Freshen the palate with an Orange Sorbet or Lemon Granita and complete your meal with something light, such as Fruit Cheese Dessert.

The Italian ingredients mentioned in the recipes are readily available in most supermarkets or delicatessens, although, of course, some of the fresh fruits and vegetables are seasonal. The following is a list of ingredients that may require a little explanation. To begin the list, here is a selection of ingredients that are useful to keep in the kitchen cupboard:

Anchovies: Used on pizzas and in sauces, tinned anchovies, preserved in brine or olive oil, are a useful stand-by to add extra flavor to your cooking.

Tomatoes and Tomato Purée: Fresh Italian plum tomatoes are the best choice for rich, juicy sauces, but for a good substitute, use the tinned variety. To thicken sauces and to add more flavor, use concentrated tomato purée, available in cans or tubes, and store in the refrigerator once opened.

Capers: The piquant flavor of capers can be used to liven up otherwise bland-flavored dishes. Capers are preserved in jars in vinegar or brine and should be drained well before using.

Nuts: Pine nuts and pistachios are widely used in both savory and sweet dishes. Although rather expensive, pine nuts are invaluable in Italian cooking and the best example is demonstrated in the distinctive flavor of Pesto Sauce. Shelled pistachios add color, bite and a delicate fragrance to ice creams and other desserts.

Dried Cèpe Mushrooms: Also known as *Porcini*, these wild mushrooms are available during the Fall. However, when fresh cèpes are out of season, dried can be substituted, as they are full of flavor. First, soak the cèpes in water for about 30 minutes, then drain and slice thinly.

Flour: If you decide to make your own pasta or pizza, use the strong variety of flour, usually sold for bread making, rather than all-purpose flour.

Rice: Italian rice is shorter and fatter in appearance than long grain rice, with a creamier consistency. It is also known as Arborio or Risotto Rice.

Olive Oil: The wide choice of olive oils can be confusing. Always buy the best olive oil that you can afford. Olive oil contains no cholestrol and is therefore a healthier alternative to animal fats. 'Cold-pressed' oil, recognised by its green color, is more expensive than a 'virgin' oil, but particularly suitable for salad dressings. Store olive oil in a cool, dark place, but not in the refrigerator, where it will go cloudy.

FRESH ITALIAN PRODUCE

Basil: The sweet scent of fresh basil is quite unique when used in sauces and salads. It is a great companion to tomato dishes.

Marjoram: When fresh marjoram is unavailable, oregano can be substituted, as it comes from the same family.

Parsley: Flat-leafed Italian parsley makes an attractive garnish or flavoring for fish dishes, soups, stews and sauces.

Salad Leaves: Add a variety of shapes and colors to your salad bowl with the wide range of Italian salad leaves available. Whichever you buy, it should be fresh, with a good color. Lettuce is best eaten fresh, although most types will keep in the salad drawer of the refrigerator for up to 2 days.

CHEESES

Fontina: This is an excellent table, as well as cooking cheese. Slightly nutty in taste, it is reminiscent of a Swiss Gruyère.

Gorgonzola: One of Italy's greatest cheeses, Gorgonzola is similar to Roquefort and Stilton. Although strong in smell, it should not be overpowering in flavor, more rich without being sharp.

Mascarpone: Think of clotted cream and then you will know Mascarpone. This is more of a dessert cheese, with a smooth and slightly sweet flavor. It should be eaten when it is very fresh.

Mozzarella: Mozzarella cheese is used mainly for cooking, as it has good binding properties. It is perhaps best known as the traditional pizza topping or in the classic Mozzarella & Tomato Salad. It has a mild creamy flavor and immaculate white color.

Parmesan: For the best flavor, buy a piece of fresh Parmesan and grate it yourself at home. Grated Parmesan is a basic ingredient of Italian cooking for the very good reason that it does not form threads as it melts. Grated, it is added to soups, sprinkled over pasta and rice, and used as a seasoning in vegetable and polenta dishes. It is also good on salads.

Pecorino: A semi-hard cheese made from ewes' milk, Pecorino can be used in the same way as Parmesan cheese.

Ricotta: Ricotta cheese is unsalted and relatively low in fat. It may be eaten plain, dressed with a light vinaigrette or used as a filling for gnocchi or ravioli. It is sometimes flavored with chocolate.

MEATS

Parma Ham: A cured meat, also known as *Prosciutto Di Parma*. Buy wafer thin slices to make a wonderful appetizer wrapped around avocado, melon or figs.

Salami: There are numerous sizes, shapes and flavors to choose from. Serve a selection of salamis with cheeses as an antipasti.

Mortadella: This is a very large Italian sausage, traditionally made from pork. Mortadella studded with chopped pistachio nuts is also available.

PASTA

There are endless shapes, sizes, colors and ways of serving pasta. Whilst dried pasta is more convenient, the flavor of fresh pasta is incomparable. Pasta should be cooked until it is 'al dente', which literally means 'firm to the bite'. Fresh pasta is ready in minutes, whereas dried pasta takes longer and the length of time depends on the size, so always follow the instructions on the package. Serve pasta tossed with your favorite sauce, or simply with a knob of butter and some freshly grated parmesan.

As the Italians say, 'Con gusto!' (Enjoy your meal!)

SOUPS

STRACCIATELLA

5 cups well-flavored chicken stock
2 eggs
3 tablespoons freshly grated Parmesan cheese
1 tablespoon semolina
2 teaspoons chopped fresh parsley
Pinch grated nutmeg
Salt to taste

Bring stock to a boil in a large saucepan. Meanwhile, beat eggs in a medium-size bowl. Stir in cheese, semolina, parsley and nutmeg. Season with salt.

When stock comes to a bubbling boil, pour in egg mixture, stirring constantly.

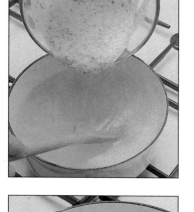

Reduce heat and simmer 2 to 3 minutes. Egg will form long threads but may look like small flakes in broth. Serve at once while hot.

Makes 4 servings.

PAVIA SOUP

5 cups chicken consommé
1/3 cup butter
2 slices firm bread
1/4 cup freshly grated Parmesan cheese (3/4 oz.)
12 quail eggs
Flat-leaf parsley to garnish
Additional freshly grated Parmesan cheese, if desired

Simmer consommé in a large saucepan. Melt butter in a large skillet. Fry bread on both sides until golden, then cut each slice in 6 pieces. Sprinkle fried bread with grated cheese.

Carefully break quail eggs into consommé, cooking 3 or 4 at a time. When set, remove eggs with a slotted spoon onto pieces of fried bread.

Place 3 pieces of fried bread with quail eggs in each soup bowl, then strain hot consommé into each. Garnish with parsley and serve with grated cheese, if desired.

Makes 4 servings.

AVGOLÉMONO

5 cups chicken stock
Salt and pepper to taste
1/3 cup long-grain white rice
2 eggs
Finely grated peel 1/2 lemon
Juice 1 lemon
3 tablespoons chopped fresh parsley
Thin lemon slices and fresh flat-leaf parsley
    leaves to garnish

Bring stock to a boil in a large saucepan.
Season with salt and pepper. Stir in rice,
cover and simmer 15 minutes or until rice is
tender.

In a small bowl, beat eggs and lemon peel and
juice. Whisk a ladleful of hot stock into egg
mixture, then pour mixture back into stock,
stirring constantly.

Reheat over low heat until soup thickens and
looks creamy. Do not allow to boil. Stir in
chopped parsley. Garnish with lemon slices
and parsley leaves and serve at once. Or serve
soup cold, if desired.

Makes 4 to 6 servings.

PASSATELLI

5 cups well-flavored chicken stock
4 eggs
1 cup freshly grated Parmesan cheese (3 oz.)
1 cup fine dry white bread crumbs
1/4 teaspoon grated nutmeg
2 tablespoons butter, softened
Salt and pepper to taste

Bring stock to a boil in a large saucepan.

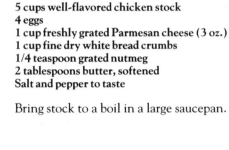

Beat eggs in a medium-size bowl. Stir in
cheese, bread crumbs, nutmeg and butter.
Season with salt and pepper. Mix to make a
stiff paste.

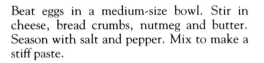

Press paste through a colander into boiling
stock. Cook 1 to 2 minutes or until threads of
noodles rise to surface. Remove from heat
and let stand 5 minutes before serving.

Makes 4 servings.

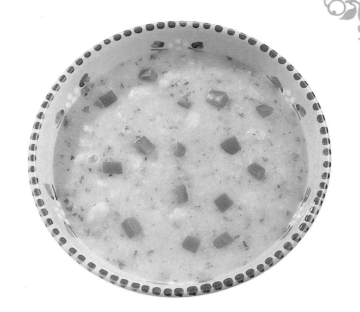

—ITALIAN BEAN & PASTA SOUP—

—WHITE BEAN SOUP—

2 tablespoons olive oil
1 medium-size onion, finely chopped
1 garlic clove, crushed
2 celery stalks, finely chopped
1 carrot, finely diced
1 tablespoon tomato paste
5 cups beef stock
1 (15-oz.) can red kidney beans, drained
3 ozs. small pasta shapes
4 ozs. frozen green peas
Salt and pepper to taste

Heat oil in a large saucepan. Add onion, garlic, celery and carrot. Stir and cook gently 5 minutes.

8 ozs. navy or cannellini beans, soaked overnight
3-3/4 cups chicken stock
3-3/4 cups water
Salt and pepper to taste
2 tablespoons olive oil
1 garlic clove, crushed
2 tablespoons chopped fresh parsley
1 tablespoon diced red bell pepper and 1
    tablespoon diced green bell pepper to garnish
Additional olive oil, if desired

Drain beans. In a large saucepan, combine drained beans, stock and water.

Add tomato paste, stock and beans. Bring to a boil and simmer 10 minutes.

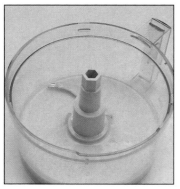

Bring to a boil. Half-cover pan and simmer 2 to 2-1/2 hours or until beans are tender. In a food processor fitted with a metal blade or a blender, process 1/2 of beans to a puree, or press through a sieve set over a bowl. Stir puree back into remaining beans.

Add pasta and peas and cook another 7 minutes or until pasta is just cooked. Season with salt and pepper.

Makes 4 to 6 servings.

Heat oil in a small saucepan. Gently cook garlic until soft. Do not allow to brown. Stir garlic and parsley into soup and reheat slowly. Meanwhile, blanch diced bell peppers in boiling water 2 minutes and drain. Garnish soup with bell peppers. If desired, pour additional oil over soup.

Makes 4 to 6 servings.

—ZUCCHINI & TOMATO SOUP—

2 tablespoons butter
1 medium-size onion, finely chopped
12 ozs. zucchini, coarsely grated
1 garlic clove, crushed
2-1/2 cups vegetable stock
1 (14-oz.) can chopped tomatoes
2 tablespoons chopped fresh mixed herbs, if
    desired
Salt and pepper to taste
1/4 cup whipping cream and fresh basil leaves to
    garnish

Melt butter in a large saucepan. Cook onion
in butter over medium heat until soft. Stir in
zucchini and garlic and cook 4 to 5 minutes.

Stir in stock and tomatoes with juice. Bring
to a boil and simmer 15 minutes.

Stir in herbs, if desired, and season with salt
and pepper. Garnish with dollops of whipping cream and basil leaves.

Makes 4 servings.

—PISTOU—

1 tablespoon olive oil
1 medium-size onion, chopped
5 cups water
1 small potato, diced
2 carrots, sliced
2 stalks celery, finely sliced
Bouquet garni
2 small zucchini, sliced
6 ozs. green beans, cut in short lengths
1 oz. broken spaghetti or pasta shells
Salt and pepper to taste

Pistou:
3 garlic cloves
1/4 cup chopped fresh basil leaves
Salt to taste
1/2 cup freshly grated Parmesan cheese (1-1/2
    ozs.)
2 medium-size tomatoes, peeled, seeded, chopped
1/4 cup olive oil

Heat 1 tablespoon oil in a large saucepan.
Cook onion in oil until onion is just beginning to color. Pour in water and bring to a
boil. Add potato, carrots, celery and bouquet
garni. Simmer 10 minutes. Add zucchini,
green beans and pasta and simmer uncovered
10 to 15 minutes or until tender.

Meanwhile, to prepare pistou, pound garlic
and basil in a mortar with a pestle. Season
with salt. Gradually add cheese until mixture
becomes a stiff paste, then add about 1/3 of
tomatoes. Continue adding cheese and
tomatoes alternately, then slowly work in
remaining oil to make a thick sauce. Remove
bouquet garni from soup. Season with salt
and pepper. Serve soup with pistou.

Makes 4 to 6 servings.

PESTO SOUP

MINESTRONE

1/4 cup plus 3 tablespoons olive oil
1 small onion, finely chopped
12 ounces zucchini, diced
1/2 cup rissotto rice
5 cups hot chicken stock
Salt and pepper to taste
1 oz. fresh basil leaves
1/4 cup pine nuts
2 garlic cloves
1/4 teaspoon salt
1/2 cup freshly grated Parmesan cheese

Parmesan Croutons:
2 tablespoons butter
2 slices bread

2 tablespoons olive oil
1 medium-size onion, chopped
1 garlic clove, crushed
1 small leek, sliced
2 carrots, diced
2 stalks celery, sliced
7-1/2 cups chicken or beef stock
1 tablespoon tomato paste
1 (14-oz.) can navy beans, drained
3 tomatoes, peeled, seeded, chopped
2 oz. green beans, cut in short lengths
2 cups shredded cabbage
1 oz. soup pasta
Salt and pepper to taste
2 tablespoons chopped fresh parsley
Freshly grated Parmesan cheese to garnish

Heat 2 tablespoons of oil in a large saucepan. Gently cook onion and zucchini 3 to 4 minutes or until softened. Stir in rice and coat grains with oil. Pour in hot stock and bring to a boil. Simmer 10 minutes or until rice is tender. Season with salt and pepper. Meanwhile, to prepare pesto sauce, process remaining olive oil, basil leaves, pine nuts, garlic and 1/4 teaspoon salt to a puree in a blender. Transfer mixture to a small bowl and beat in 1/2 of cheese.

Heat oil in a large saucepan. Cook onion, garlic and leek over low heat 5 minutes. Stir in carrots, celery, stock, tomato paste and drained beans and bring to a simmer. Cover and cook 30 minutes. Stir in tomatoes and green beans and simmer 10 minutes.

To prepare croutons, beat remaining cheese and butter in a small bowl. Toast bread on both sides. Spread toast with cheese-butter and broil until melted and golden. Cut out fancy shapes or remove crusts and dice. Stir 1 heaping tablespoon of pesto sauce into soup. Refrigerate remaining pesto sauce for another use. Garnish soup with croutons.

Makes 4 to 5 servings.

Stir in cabbage and pasta. Season with salt and pepper. Cook 10 minutes or until pasta is tender. Stir in parsley. Garnish with cheese.

Makes 6 servings.

GARLIC SOUP

FLORENTINE SOUP

3 tablespoons butter
6 garlic cloves
1/4 cup all-purpose flour
2-1/2 cups chicken stock
2/3 cup dry white wine
1 teaspoon dried leaf thyme
Salt and pepper to taste
1 egg yolk
2/3 cup half and half
3/4 cup ground almonds
Seedless green grapes, cut in half, to garnish

Melt butter in a large saucepan. Slightly crush garlic. Cook garlic in butter over low heat 3 to 4 minutes or until golden.

Stir in flour, then gradually blend in stock. Stir in wine and thyme. Season with salt and pepper and simmer 10 minutes. In a large bowl, beat egg yolk and half and half. Strain stock mixture into bowl, whisking constantly.

Clean pan and return mixture to clean pan. Stir in almonds and reheat without boiling. Garnish soup with grapes.

Makes 4 servings.

1-1/2 lbs. fresh spinach
1/4 cup butter
1 shallot, chopped
1/4 cup all-purpose flour
2-1/2 cups chicken or vegetable stock
Salt and pepper to taste
1/4 teaspoon grated nutmeg
2-1/2 cups milk
3 tablespoons whipping cream
1/4 cup whipping cream and 2 very small eggs, hard cooked, sliced, to garnish

Pick over spinach, discarding stalks, and wash thoroughly.

Cook spinach in a large saucepan over medium heat until tender. Pour spinach into a colander set over a bowl and press out as much water as possible. Melt butter in a large saucepan. Cook shallot in butter until soft. Blend in flour and cook 1 minute. Add spinach and stock and simmer 15 minutes. Season with salt and pepper. Add nutmeg.

In a food processor fitted with a metal blade or a blender, process soup mixture to a puree. Clean pan and return puree to clean pan. Add milk and reheat gently. Just before serving, stir in 3 tablespoons whipping cream. To serve, swirl 1 tablespoon of whipping cream on each portion of soup and garnish with hard-cooked egg slices.

Makes 4 servings.

— ITALIAN MEATBALL SOUP —

Meatballs:
6 ozs. very lean ground beef
1 small egg
1 teaspoon finely chopped onion
1 tablespoon fresh bread crumbs
2 teaspoons chopped fresh parsley
Salt and pepper to taste
Pinch grated nutmeg

Soup:
3-3/4 cups beef consommé
1 tablespoon butter
1 large carrot, julienned in thin matchstick strips
1 leek, shredded
1 small turnip, julienned in thin matchstick strips
Salt and pepper to taste

To prepare meatballs, in a medium-size bowl, combine all meatball ingredients. With dampened hands, roll ground beef in 16 small walnut-size balls. Bring a pan of water to a boil. Lower heat to simmer and drop in meatballs. Gently cook 10 minutes. Remove meatballs with a slotted spoon and set aside.

In a large saucepan, combine 2/3 cup of consommé, butter and vegetables. Cover and cook over medium heat 5 minutes. Add remaining consommé and meatballs. Bring to a boil and simmer 2 to 3 minutes or until meatballs are reheated. Season with salt and pepper.

Makes 4 servings.

— TOMATO & PASTA SOUP —

8 medium-size tomatoes
1/4 cup butter
1 medium-size onion, finely chopped (1/2 cup)
1/3 cup ditalini or elbow macaroni (2 oz.)
1 quart chicken stock
Pinch of saffron
Pinch of chilli powder
Salt
Fresh parsley, if desired

Put tomatoes into a bowl. Cover with boiling water 1 minute. Drain. Cover with cold water 1 minute. Drain. Remove and discard skins and chop tomatoes. In a large saucepan, melt butter. Add onion. Cook until beginning to soften. Add ditalini; cook, stirring, 2 minutes. Add tomatoes. Add stock and saffron. Bring to a boil; reduce heat. Cover; simmer until ditalini is just tender to the bite. Stir in chili powder and salt to taste. Garnish with parsley, if desired.

Makes 4 servings.

APPETIZERS

PROSCIUTTO ROULADES

2 oz. ricotta cheese (1/4 cup)
2 oz. Stilton cheese, crumbled
1 tablespoon dairy sour cream
12 very thin slices prosciutto, coppa salami or
**   lean cooked ham**
1 pear
Lemon juice
Lime slices and dill sprigs, if desired

In a small bowl, thoroughly blend ricotta cheese, Stilton cheese and sour cream. Spread evenly on prosciutto, salami or ham slices, spreading mixture almost to edges.

Peel, quarter and core pear, then cut each quarter lengthwise in 3 thin slices. Brush slices lightly with lemon juice to prevent darkening. Place a pear slice on each cheese-topped prosciutto slice.

SMOKED SALMON
& AVOCADO ROLL

1 bunch watercress
3 green onions, very finely chopped
1 tablespoon olive oil
1 teaspoon prepared horseradish
Salt and pepper
1 avocado
Juice of 1/2 lemon
3 cooked green lasagne noodles
3 oz. smoked salmon, thinly sliced
1/4 cup mayonnaise
1/4 cup crème fraîche
1 tablespoon chopped fresh dill weed
Milk as needed
Lemon peel strips, if desired
Fresh dill, if desired

In a saucepan of boiling water, blanch watercress 10 seconds. Drain; refresh in a bowl of cold water. Squeeze gently in a cloth to dry. Chop fine. In a small bowl, mix together watercress, green onions, olive oil, horseradish, salt and pepper. Halve and pit avocado; peel. Cut in lengthwise slices. Toss avocado in lemon juice. Spread a little watercress mixture over each sheet of lasagne. Lay a slice of smoked salmon on each sheet. Arrange avocado slices in a line down the length of the middle of each sheet. Starting with a long side of pasta, roll up jelly-roll fashion. Wrap each roll in plastic wrap. Chill 2 hours. In a bowl, mix together mayonnaise, crème fraîche, dill weed, salt and pepper. Add a little milk, if necessary, to make a pouring consistency. Cut each roll diagonally in slices 3/4-inch wide. Garnish with lemon peel strips and dill, if desired. Serve with dill sauce.

Makes 4 to 6 first course servings.

Roll up prosciutto slices, cover and refrigerate until ready to serve. Garnish with lime slice and dill sprig, if desired.

Makes 12.

Variation: Substitute an apple or fresh figs for the pear. Peel and slice figs before using.

BASIL-CHEESE TOASTS

2 tomatoes
1 (2-oz.) can flat anchovy fillets
10 slices French bread
1 cup shredded Gruyère cheese (4 oz)
Freshly ground pepper to taste
1/4 cup shredded fresh basil leaves
1/4 cup olive oil
Basil sprigs

Thinly slice tomatoes. If tomatoes are large, cut each slice in half. Drain anchovies and cut in strips. Set tomatoes and anchovies aside.

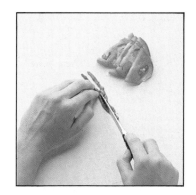

Lightly oil a large, shallow baking dish. Pre-heat oven to 400F (200C). Arrange bread slices in oiled baking dish; sprinkle evenly with cheese. Arrange anchovy strips over cheese; top each bread slice with 1 or 2 tomato slices.

Sprinkle with pepper and some of basil. Drizzle oil over all. Bake 10 to 15 minutes or until bread is crisp and cheese is melted. Sprinkle with remaining basil and garnish with basil sprigs. Serve hot.

Makes 10.

RICOTTA-CHEESE BALLS

2 lbs. ricotta cheese (4 cups), well chilled
1 red bell pepper, seeded, finely chopped
1/4 cup finely chopped mixed fresh herbs
(including some green onion, if desired)
1/4 cup black sesame seeds or finely chopped
pistachio nuts
1 teaspoon salt

Line a baking sheet or tray with plastic wrap. Using a small ice-cream scoop or a spoon, shape ricotta cheese into 24 equal balls. Divide ricotta balls into 3 groups of 8 balls each. Roll 1 group in chopped bell pepper.

Roll second group of balls in chopped herbs.

Mix sesame seeds or pistachios and salt, spread on a sheet of wax paper. Roll remaining 8 balls in nut or seed mixture. Arrange all balls on lined baking sheets; cover and refrigerate until ready to serve. To serve, arrange ricotta balls in rows on a platter.

Makes 24.

Tip: Black sesame seeds are available in Asian grocery stores.

AIOLI & CRUDITÉS

BAGNA CAUDA

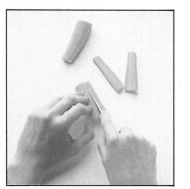

4 garlic cloves
About 1/2 teaspoon salt
2 egg yolks
1 cup olive oil
Juice of 1/2 lemon
Crisp raw vegetables, such as carrot sticks, celery
sticks, small whole radishes, cauliflowerets,
edible-pod peas, cucumber sticks, blanched
fresh asparagus spears and green onions.

Press garlic through a garlic press into a bowl.
Add 1/2 teaspoon salt and egg yolks; beat well
with a whisk. Add 1 or 2 drops oil and whisk
well.

Gradually add about 2 more tablespoons oil,
whisking constantly. Then, still whisking
constantly, add remaining oil in a thin
stream. If mixture becomes too thick, add a
little hot water. When all oil has been added,
whisk in lemon juice and season with additional salt, if needed. Cover aioli and
refrigerate until ready to use.

Prepare the uncooked vegetables; cut the
carrots in 3-inch sticks, slice the cucumber
and trim the celery, radishes, cauliflowers
and green onions. To serve, spoon aioli into
a serving bowl and place in center of a large
platter. Arrange vegetables around aioli; dip
vegetables in aioli before eating.

Makes about 1 cup aioli.

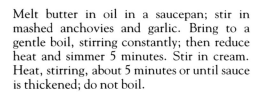

Crisp raw vegetables, such as 2 or 3 carrots,
edible-pod peas and 1/2 cauliflower
1 (2-oz.) can flat anchovy fillets, drained
1/2 cup butter
1/2 cup olive oil or vegetable oil
4 garlic cloves, crushed
1/2 pint whipping cream (1 cup)
Crusty bread, sliced

Cut carrots in 4-inch pieces, then cut in thin
strips. Separate cauliflower into flowerets;
trim and rinse the edible-pod peas. Mash the
anchovies.

Melt butter in oil in a saucepan; stir in
mashed anchovies and garlic. Bring to a
gentle boil, stirring constantly; then reduce
heat and simmer 5 minutes. Stir in cream.
Heat, stirring, about 5 minutes or until sauce
is thickened; do not boil.

To serve, pour hot anchovy sauce into a
warmed bowl or a chafing dish. Arrange
vegetables and a basket of bread around
sauce. Let guests spear vegetables with
wooden skewers, then dip in sauce and eat
with a slice of bread to catch the drips.

Makes about 2 cups sauce.

SWEET PEPPER SALAD

2 large red bell peppers
2 large yellow bell peppers
6 tablespoons extra-virgin olive oil
2 garlic cloves, peeled
Salt and black pepper to taste
Ripe olives and flat-leaf parsley sprigs

Preheat broiler. Place all bell peppers in a shallow baking pan and broil until skins are blistered and blackened, turning often to char evenly. Remove peppers from pan, place in a plastic bag and close bag tightly. Let peppers sweat 10 to 15 minutes, then remove and discard skins, stems and seeds. Cut flesh into strips; arrange in a shallow dish. Drizzle oil over peppers. Cut garlic into thin slivers and scatter it over peppers; season with salt and pepper. Cover and let marinate 24 hours. To serve, garnish with olives and parsley sprigs.

Makes 4 to 6 servings.

MIXED MELON SALAD

1 honeydew melon
1 cantaloupe
1/4 watermelon
1/2 cup seedless green grapes
1 tablespoon superfine sugar
1 tablespoon tarragon vinegar
2 tablespoons vegetable oil
2 teaspoons chopped fresh mint
1 teaspoon chopped fresh tarragon
2 slightly firm avocados
Sprigs of mint and chervil to garnish

Cut honeydew melon and cantaloupe in half and remove seeds. Remove seeds from watermelon. Using a melon baller, scoop out melon balls; place in a large serving bowl and add grapes. In a small bowl, mix sugar, vinegar and oil and pour over fruit. Stir in chopped herbs. Cover and chill 1 hour. Cut avocados in half and remove pits. Using a melon baller, scoop out pulp and add to fruit; mix well. Garnish with sprigs of mint and chervil.

Makes 4 servings.

MARINATED ARTICHOKES

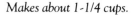

1 (14 oz.) can artichoke hearts packed in water, drained
6 tablespoons olive oil or vegetable oil
Freshly ground pepper to taste
3 tablespoons chopped mixed fresh herbs such as parsley, basil and oregano
Lemon juice and salt to taste
Toast rounds, if desired.

Rinse artichoke hearts well in cold water. Drain, pat dry and cut lengthwise in halves or quarters.

Place in a bowl and add oil, pepper and herbs. Mix well. Cover and refrigerate at least 4 hours or until ready to serve. For longer storage, place artichokes in a jar, making sure they are covered with oil; cover tightly and refrigerate up to 2 weeks. To serve, bring to room temperature. Stir well; season with lemon juice and salt. Offer wooden picks for picking up artichoke; or serve artichokes on toast rounds. Provide small napkins. If desired, add artichokes to salads.

Makes about 1-1/4 cups.

Variations: For added bite, mix a few slivers of fresh, red hot chili into the marinade. If you're a garlic lover, add a crushed garlic clove.

AVOCADO WITH MASCARPONE

4 avocados, ripe but firm, halved
3 tablespoons freshly squeezed lemon juice
4 oz. mascarpone cheese
1 or 2 teaspoons French-style mustard
1 garlic clove, crushed
Few drops hot pepper sauce
Salt and pepper, to taste

To Garnish:
1/4 cup (1 oz.) sliced almonds
Parsley sprigs
Chive flowers (optional)

Carefully scoop out avocado using a teaspoon, making sure skins remain whole; set skins aside. Roughly chop the flesh, put into a bowl and sprinkle with 1 tablespoon of the lemon juice, to prevent discoloration.

In a separate bowl, blend cheese with mustard to taste, garlic and remaining lemon juice. Season with hot pepper sauce, salt and pepper. Add chopped avocado and mix in carefully. Pile into avocado shells and chill about 20 minutes.

Garnish with almonds, parsley and chive flowers if available, and serve in individual dishes.

Makes 8 servings.

Note: This tasty dish can be served with French bread, as a light lunch for 4 people.

NECTARINES WITH PROSCIUTTO

Greens of your choice
2 nectrines
4 oz. thinly sliced prosciutto
3 tablespoons virgin olive oil
5 teaspoons sunflower oil
1 tablespoon raspberry vinegar
Fresh raspberries

Line 4 plates with greens. Slice nectarines. Halve each slice of prosciutto. Wrap each nectarine slice in prosciutto; arrange atop greens. Whisk together olive oil, sunflower oil and vinegar; drizzle over salad. Garnish with raspberries and serve.

Makes 4 first course servings.

RISOTTO CON FUNGHI

1 oz. dried cepes (porcini)
1/2 cup butter
1 small onion, finely chopped
2 cups short-grain rice, such as pearl
4 oz. fresh mushrooms (*see Note*), quartered or sliced
2/3 cup dry white wine
5 cups hot chicken stock
3 tablespoons freshly grated Parmesan cheese
Salt and pepper, to taste

To Garnish:
Chopped parsley
Parsley sprigs

To Serve:
Tomato salad

Place cepes in a small bowl; cover with warm water and let soak 20 minutes. Drain; rinse well to remove any grit. Chop coarsely.

In a saucepan, melt 1/4 cup butter. Add onion and sauté about 5 minutes or until golden. Stir in rice and fresh mushrooms and cook 2 to 3 minutes or until rice is translucent. Add wine and cepes; cook about 3 minutes or until

wine is absorbed. Reduce heat, add 2-1/2 cups stock, cover and simmer about 10 minutes or until almost all stock has been absorbed.

Add 1-1/4 cups more stock to pan and continue to cook, checking periodically and adding more stock as needed, until rice is tender and all liquid has been absorbed. Total cooking time will range from 20 to 30 minutes. Stir in remaining 1/4 cup butter, cheese, salt and pepper.

Transfer risotto to warmed serving plates and garnish with chopped parsley and parsley sprigs. Serve with a tomato salad.

Makes 4 to 6 servings.

Note: Dried cepes give this dish an incomparable flavor; for visual appeal and texture, I like to add fresh mushrooms. Use sliced fresh cepes (if available) or quartered button mushrooms. Avoid brown mushrooms, since they tend to color the risotto gray.

CRISPY PESTO SHRIMP

12 cooked peeled jumbo shrimp
6 large slices white bread
1/4 cup butter
1 clove garlic
1 tablespoon plus 1 teaspoon pesto sauce
1 teaspoon finely grated lemon peel
1/4 teaspoon salt
1/4 teaspoon ground black pepper
Lemon triangles and lemon balm leaves to
    garnish

Cut each shrimp in half across width. Cut crusts off bread. Using a rolling pin, roll each slice flat.

In a small bowl, beat butter until soft and smooth. Stir in garlic, pesto sauce, lemon peel, salt and pepper. Beat until smooth and well blended. Spread both sides of each slice of bread with butter mixture and cut each slice in 4 triangles.

Place a shrimp in center of each bread triangle. Fold 2 points to center and secure with a wooden pick. Arrange on a grid in a grill pan and broil under a moderately hot grill until bread is lightly browned. Garnish with lemon triangles and lemon balm leaves and serve hot.

Makes 24 pieces.

ASPARAGUS IN CHICORY LEAVES

8 oz. asparagus spears, trimmed
3 heads chicory
1 (8 oz.) pkg. cream cheese
3 slices proscuitto or parma ham
Tangerine wedges and dill sprigs to garnish

Marinade:
1 tangerine
1/2 clove garlic, crushed
1/4 teaspoon salt
1/4 teaspoon ground black pepper
1/2 teaspoon Dijon-style mustard
2 teaspoons honey
1 tablespoon plus 1 teaspoon olive oil
2 teaspoons chopped fresh tarragon

Half-fill a shallow skillet with water; bring to a boil. Add asparagus and cook 3 to 4 minutes or until spears are tender. Drain and cool in a shallow dish.

To prepare marinade, using a zester, cut peel of tangerine into fine strips; squeeze juice into a bowl. Add garlic, salt, pepper, mustard, honey, oil and tarragon and beat with a wooden spoon until thoroughly blended. Pour over asparagus, cover and chill for at least 1 hour.

Separate chicory leaves and cut in 1-inch lengths. Spread a little cream cheese onto each leaf. Cut asparagus spears in 1-inch lengths; place a piece of asparagus onto each chicory leaf. Cut proscuitto or ham in thin strips and wrap a piece around each chicory leaf. Garnish with tangerine wedges and dill sprigs.

Makes 48 pieces.

DEEP-FRIED CAMBAZOLA

8 oz. firm cambazola (or similar blue brie-
   type cheese)
1/2 cup all-purpose flour
Salt and pepper, to taste
2 eggs
1/2 cup dry bread crumbs
Vegetable oil for deep-frying

To Garnish:
4 plums, sliced

To Serve:
1/2 cup Chinese plum sauce

Using a small sharp knife, remove white rind and cut cheese into 3/4 inch cubes.

Season flour with salt and pepper. Beat eggs in one bowl; put bread crumbs in another.

Dip cheese cubes in seasoned flour, coating each piece well; shake off excess. Next dip in beaten eggs, then bread crumbs to coat well, firmly pat-ting them into place. Refrigerate 20 minutes.

Fill a deep-fryer one-third full with vegetable oil and heat to 360F (180C) or until a 1-inch bread cube turns golden brown in 1 minute. Using a slotted spoon, carefully lower cheese cubes one at a time into hot oil; do not overfill pan – cook cubes in batches. Deep-fry 3 to 4 minutes or until golden brown; remove with a slotted spoon and drain on paper towels. Serve immediately on warmed plates; the melted cheese oozes out on standing. Garnish with sliced plums and a little Chinese plum sauce.

Makes 4 to 5 servings.

Note: Chinese plum sauce is available from Chinese stores, some super-markets and delicatessens.

TOMATO & BASIL SORBET

4 large fresh tomatoes
1 (8-oz.) can ready-cut tomatoes
1 teaspoon sugar
2 teaspoons tomato paste
2 teaspoons wine vinegar
1/2 teaspoon onion salt
1 teaspoon Worcestershire sauce
2 teaspoons chopped fresh basil
1 tablespoon plus 1 teaspoon vodka

Remove tops from fresh tomatoes and scoop out all seeds and flesh, leaving 4 shells. Place shells and tops in freezer. In a blender or food processor fitted with the metal blade, process tomato flesh and seeds and remaining ingre-dients 2 minutes. Pour into a plastic container and freeze. When frozen to a slush, process in blender or food pro-cessor until slightly softened and pale. Using a pastry bag fitted with a plain nozzle, pipe sorbet into frozen shells. Return to freezer until firm.

Makes 4 servings.

Note: Serve with hot buttered toast.

MARINATED MUSHROOMS

1 lb. small fresh mushrooms
1 cup water
2 teaspoons salt
1/2 cup distilled white vinegar
1 bay leaf
Few thyme sprigs
1 garlic clove
2 tablespoons olive oil
Sliced green onion or mild red onion, if desired
Finely chopped parsley
Peel of 1 lemon, cut in thin strips

PROSCIUTTO WITH FIGS

4 oz. prosciutto, sliced very thin
4 fresh figs
4 fig or vine leaves
1 teaspoon honey
1 tablespoon plus 1 teaspoon fresh lime
  juice
1 tablespoon plus 2 teaspoons olive oil
1 teaspoon pink peppercorns, slightly
  crushed
Shredded lime peel to garnish

Trim any excess fat from prosciutto and cut in half lengthwise. Cut figs in quarters. Arrange fig leaves on individual plates and pleat prosciutto on top. Place figs in prosciutto nest. In a small bowl, combine honey, lime juice, olive oil and peppercorns and whisk well. Spoon over figs and ham and garnish with shredded lime peel.

Makes 4 servings.

Trim mushroom stems. Wipe mushrooms with a cloth dipped in cold acidulated water (1-1/2 teaspoons lemon juice or distilled white vinegar to 2 cups water). Place mushrooms in a heatproof bowl.

In a saucepan, combine 1 cup water, salt, vinegar, bay leaf, thyme sprigs, garlic and oil. Bring to a boil; pour over mushrooms. Cool, then cover and refrigerate at least 12 hours or up to 3 days.

To serve, drain mushrooms and place in a serving bowl. Discard bay leaf, thyme and garlic. If desired, gently mix in sliced onion. Sprinkle with parsley and lemon peel. If desired, offer wooden picks for picking up mushrooms; provide small napkins.

Makes about 3 cups.

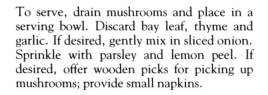

SALADS & DRESSINGS

─ITALIAN SEAFOOD SALAD─

2 lbs. live mussels, scrubbed, de-bearded
1 lb. small live hard-shell clams, scrubbed
1 tablespoon extra-virgin olive oil
3 small whole squid, cleaned and prepared
6 oz. shelled, deveined cooked shrimp
Dressing, see below
Flat-leaf parsley sprigs
Lemon wedges, if desired

Dressing:
5 tablespoons extra-virgin olive oil
2 tablespoons lemon juice
1 tablespoon chopped parsley
1 garlic clove, finely chopped
1 tablespoon capers, drained
Salt and pepper, to taste

In a large saucepan, combine mussels
and 1 cup water and bring to a boil.
Reduce heat, cover and simmer 5 to 10
minutes or until shells open. Remove
from heat. Discard any mussels that
remain closed. When mussels are cool
enough to handle, remove them from
shells. Set aside. Then cook clams and
remove from shells as directed for
mussels. Heat oil in a heavy skillet, add
squid rings and tentacles and sauté 2 to
3 minutes or until opaque. Turn into a
bowl and add mussels, clams and
shrimp. To prepare Dressing. Stir together all ingredients. pour over seafood mixture, cover and refrigerate 2
hours, stirring occasionally. Garnish
salad with parsley and, if desired,
lemon wedges before serving.

Makes 4 servings.

─CAPONATA─

2 medium eggplants
Salt
1/2 cup olive oil
1 small onion, chopped
4 celery stalks, chopped
1 (about 1-lb.) can tomatoes
2 to 3 tablespoons red wine vinegar
1 tablespoon sugar
1 tablespoon capers, drained
12 pitted green olives, chopped
1 tablespoon pine nuts, lightly toasted
Salt and pepper, to taste
1 tablespoon chopped parsley

Cut eggplants into small cubes and
place in a colander. Sprinkle with salt
and set aside to drain 1 hour. Meanwhile, heat 2 tablespoons oil in a skillet
over medium heat, add onion and cook
5 minutes or until softened. Add celery
and cook 3 minutes longer. Drain
tomatoes, reserving juice; chop tomatoes. Stir chopped tomatoes and their
juice into skillet; simmer, uncovered, 5
minutes. Stir in vinegar and sugar and
simmer 15 minutes longer. Set aside.
Rinse eggplant cubes and pat dry on
paper towels. Heat remaining 6 tablespoons oil in a very large skillet, add
eggplant and cook until tender and
golden, turning often. Stir in tomato
mixture, capers, olives and pine nuts;
season with salt and pepper. Continue
to simmer 2 to 3 minutes longer. Turn
into a bowl; let cool. (For best flavor,
refrigerate 24 hours to allow flavors to
mingle.) Sprinkle with parsley before
serving.

Makes 6 servings.

Variation: For a more substantial dish,
garnish the Caponata with flaked tuna.

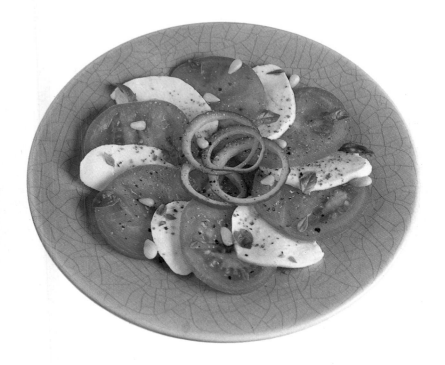

TOMATO & MOZZARELLA SALAD

—SPINACH & BACON SALAD—

2 large beefsteak tomatoes, sliced
6 oz. mozzarella cheese, sliced
1 small red onion, sliced, separated into
   rings
Salt and black pepper, to taste
1/4 cup extra-virgin olive oil
1 tablespoon fresh basil leaves
1 tablespoon pine nuts

Arrange tomato slices and cheese slices
on 4 plates. Top with onion rings.
Season with salt and pepper, then
drizzle with oil. Sprinkle with basil and
pine nuts and serve.

Makes 4 servings.

6 to 8 cups young spinach leaves, washed
   well, trimmed
2 oz. fresh button mushrooms, stems
   trimmed, sliced
3 thick slices bread, crusts removed
1/4 cup sunflower oil
1 garlic clove, crushed
6 oz. sliced bacon, chopped
2 tablespoons white wine vinegar
Freshly ground black pepper to taste

Tear spinach into bite-size pieces.
Place spinach and mushrooms in
a salad bowl. Cut bread into small
squares. Heat oil in a skillet, add bread
squares and garlic and cook until bread
is crisp and golden, turning frequently.
Remove with a slotted spoon and drain
on paper towels. Wipe out skillet with
paper towels. Add bacon and cook
about 5 minutes or until crisp and
browned. Pour bacon and its drippings
over spinach mixture. Add vinegar to
skillet with a few grinds of pepper;
bring to a boil, then immediately pour
over salad and toss. Sprinkle salad with
croutons, spoon onto plates and serve
at once.

Makes 6 servings.

CALF'S LIVER BALSAMICO

2 large (8-oz.) slices calf's liver
A few escarole leaves
A few radicchio or lollo rosso leaves
2 to 3 cups mâche (lamb's lettuce)
1/4 cup extra-virgin olive oil
1 tablespoon shredded fresh sage
2 tablespoons balsamic vinegar
Salt and pepper, to taste
1 tablespoon pine nuts

Rinse liver; trim off any membranes and large veins. Pat liver dry and cut into thin strips. Set aside. Tear escarole, radicchio or lollo rosso and mâche into smaller pieces. Arrange on 4 plates. Heat oil in a skillet. Add liver and sage and cook 2 to 3 minutes or until liver is browned on outside but still pink inside, stirring constantly. Remove liver from skillet with a slotted spoon and divide among plates. Pour vinegar into drippings in skillet; heat to warm through. Season with salt and pepper, then spoon over greens and liver on plates. Sprinkle with pine nuts and serve.

Makes 4 first-course servings.

PASTA PESTO SALAD

8 oz. dried orzo (rice-shaped pasta)
8 oz. cherry tomatoes, quartered
Pesto Dressing, see below
About 1/4 cup pine nuts, lightly toasted
Fresh basil sprigs

Pesto Dressing:
About 1 cup lightly packed fresh basil
  leaves
2 garlic cloves, peeled
About 1/4 cup pine nuts
3 tablespoons virgin olive oil
1/4 cup freshly grated Parmesan cheese
  (3/4 oz.)
3 tablespoons half and half

Following package directions, cook pasta in boiling salted water just until tender but still firm. Drain, rinse with cold water and drain again. Place in a bowl and add tomatoes. To prepare Pesto Dressing, combine basil leaves, garlic, pine nuts and oil in a blender and process until smooth. Turn into a bowl and beat in cheese and half and half. Stir dressing into pasta mixture, then transfer to a serving dish and sprinkle with toasted pine nuts. Garnish with basil sprigs.

Makes 4 side-dish servings.

ITALIAN SALAMI SALAD

1 (about 15 oz.) can navy beans or
    cannellini (white kidney beans),
    drained
1 fennel bulb, trimmed, thinly sliced
1 small green bell pepper, seeded, diced
4 oz. sliced Italian salami
Garlic Dressing see below
Shredded fresh basil
Tomato wedges
Ripe olives

Garlic Dressing:
3 tablespoons extra-virgin olive oil
1 tablespoon white wine vinegar
1 garlic clove, crushed
Salt and pepper, to taste

Combine beans, fennel and bell pepper
in a bowl. Cut salami slices into quarters and add to salad. To prepare Garlic
Dressing, stir together all dressing
ingredients. Pour dressing over salad;
toss to mix. Spoon into a serving dish
and garnish with basil, tomato wedges
and olives.

Makes 4 servings.

EGGS TONNATO

Tonnato Sauce, see below
6 large hard-cooked eggs
Pimento strips
1 (2 oz.) can flat anchovy fillets, drained
Fresh dill sprigs

Tonnato Sauce:
1 recipe mayonnaise
1 small (3-1/2 oz.) can tuna, drained
1 tablespoon lemon juice
1 tablespoon half and half or plain yogurt
1 teaspoon capers, drained, chopped

To prepare Tonnato Sauce, place
Mayonnaise in a blender along with
tuna, lemon juice and half and half or
yogurt. Process until smooth; stir in
capers. Halve eggs lengthwise and
place 3 halves on each of 4 plates.
Spoon sauce over eggs; decorate with
pimento strips. To garnish salad, halve
anchovy fillets; roll up each half and
place between eggs. Top with dill sprigs
and serve.

Makes 4 servings.

PASTA & SHRIMP SALAD

8 oz. dried small pasta shells (use part or all
   spinach shells, if desired)
12 oz. shelled, deveined cooked shrimp
4 oz. smoked salmon, cut into thin strips
Herb Dressing, see below
Fresh tarragon sprigs

Herb Dressing:
4-1/2 tablespoons virgin olive oil
1-1/2 tablespoons lemon juice
1-1/2 tablespoons tomato juice
1-1/2 tablespoons chopped parsley
1-1/2 tablespoons chopped fresh tarragon
Salt and black pepper, to taste

Following package directions, cook
pasta in boiling salted water just until
tender but still firm. Drain, rinse with
cold water and drain again. Place in a
bowl with shrimp and salmon. To prepare Herb Dressing, stir all dressing
ingredients together. Pour over salad,
toss to mix and transfer to a serving
dish. Garnish with tarragon sprigs.

Makes 4 main-dish servings.

TONNO CON FAGIOLI

1 (about (15 oz.) can cannellini (white
   kidney beans), drained
1 (about 14 oz.) can flageolets, drained
1/2 red onion, sliced
Salt and pepper, to taste
2 (6-1/2 to 7 oz.) cans tuna, drained
2 tablespoons chopped parsley
5 tablespoons extra-virgin olive oil
1 tablespoon red wine vinegar
Ripe olives
Lemon slices
Flat-leaf parsley sprigs

In a bowl, combine cannellini, flageolets and onion. Season with salt and
pepper. Add tuna, breaking it into
large flakes with a fork; stir in chopped
parsley. Stir together oil and vinegar;
season with salt and pepper. Add to
salad, tossing to mix well. Transfer to a
serving dish and garnish with olives,
lemon slices and parsley sprigs.

*Makes 4 main-course or 6 first-course
servings.*

THREE-COLORED PASTA SALAD —— CLASSIC TOMATO SALAD——

6 green onions
1 small red bell pepper, diced
1 small green bell pepper, diced
1 recipe dressing
4 cups red, green and white pasta shells
    (8 oz.)

Chop green onions until fine. In a bowl, combine green onions and bell peppers with Dressing. In a large saucepan of boiling salted water, cook pasta until just tender to the bite. Drain; rinse in cold water. Drain thoroughly. In a large bowl, mix together Dressing and pasta.

Makes 4 to 6 servings.

1 lb. firm-ripe tomatoes
1 teaspoon sugar
Salt and pepper, to taste
6 tablespoons virgin olive oil
2 tablespoons white wine vinegar
1 tablespoon snipped chives

Thinly slice tomatoes and arrange on a serving plate. Sprinkle with sugar and season with salt and pepper. Stir together oil and vinegar and spoon over salad. Sprinkle with chives, then cover and refrigerate at least 1 hour before serving.

Makes 4 servings.

Variation: Sprinkle salad with finely chopped green onion or shredded fresh basil instead of chives.

TOSSED GREEN SALAD

About 10 cups greens of your choice, such as chicory, escarole, romaine lettuce, Bibb lettuce or iceberg lettuce (include at least 2 kinds of greens)
Salt
1 garlic clove, peeled
1 tablespoon wine vinegar
1/4 teaspoon Dijon-style mustard
2 teaspoons lemon juice
1/4 cup extra-virgin olive oil
A few young spinach leaves, washed well, trimmed
1 bunch watercress, trimmed
1/2 cucumber, sliced or diced
1 medium green bell pepper, seeded, chopped
2 tablespoons chopped mixed fresh herbs, such as parsley, chervil, tarragon, summer savory or chives

Tear any large leaves of greens into smaller pieces. If not using immediately, place in a plastic bag and refrigerate until ready to use. To assemble salad, put a little salt into a wooden salad bowl. Add garlic clove; crush to a paste with salt, using back of a wooden spoon. Add vinegar, mustard and lemon juice; stir in oil and continue to mix to make an emulsion. Add greens, spinach, watercress, cucumber, bell pepper and herbs; toss well, so every leaf is coated with dressing. Serve immediately.

Makes 6 servings.

Tip: For a less garlicky flavor, rub inside of bowl with a cut garlic clove, then discard garlic. (If you do not have a wooden salad bowl, make dressing in a separate small bowl and pour over salad just before serving.)

WINTER RED SALAD

1 head oak leaf lettuce or 1 small head red leaf lettuce
1 head radicchio
1 red onion, thinly sliced
About 1-1/3 cups shredded red cabbage
About 1 cup diced cooked beets
Walnut Vinaigrette, see below
1/2 pomegranate, peel and pith removed, seeds separated

Walnut Vinaigrette:
3 tablespoons walnut oil
1-1/2 tablespoons virgin olive oil
1-1/2 tablespoons red wine vinegar
3/4 teaspoon Dijon-style mustard
Pinch of sugar
Salt and black pepper, to taste

Tear large lettuce and radicchio leaves into smaller pieces. Arrange lettuce and radicchio in a bowl. Add onion, cabbage and beets. To prepare Walnut Vinaigrette, stir together all vinaigrette ingredients. Pour vinaigrette over salad and toss. Sprinkle with pomegranate seeds and serve.

Makes 4 to 6 servings.

—ITALIAN MUSHROOM SALAD—

1 small head red oak leaf or lollo rosso
  lettuce
1/2 red onion, thinly sliced
8 oz. button mushrooms, thinly sliced
2 oz. Parmesan cheese
2 teaspoons finely chopped parsley

Lemon Dressing:
5 tablespoons virgin olive oil
Finely grated peel of 1/2 lemon
Juice of 1 small lemon
1/4 teaspoon coarse-grained mustard
Pinch of sugar
Salt and pepper, to taste

Prepare Lemon Dressing: Stir all dressing ingredients together in a small bowl, or combine in a screw-top jar and shake well. Set aside.

Tear lettuce into bite-size pieces; arrange lettuce and onion on individual serving plates. Set aside.

Place mushrooms in a large bowl. Pour dressing over them and toss well to coat. Pare cheese into wafer-thin slices and add to mushrooms, tossing lightly to mix.

Arrange mushroom mixture atop lettuce, sprinkle with parsley and serve immediately.

Makes 4 servings.

Note: The mushrooms may be left to marinate in the dressing up to 2 hours, but it's best to add the Parmesan to the salad just before serving.

——TRICOLOR PASTA SALAD——

8 oz. dried tricolor rotelle (corkscrew
  pasta)
1 tablespoon virgin olive oil
4 oz. fresh button mushrooms or wild
  mushrooms, stems trimmed, sliced
1/2 cup pitted green olives, chopped
1 (2 oz.) can flat anchovy fillets, drained,
  cut into thin strips
1 tablespoon chopped fresh oregano
3 tablespoons virgin olive oil
1-1/2 tablespoons balsamic vinegar
Salt and black pepper, to taste

Following package directions, cook pasta in boiling salted water until tender but still firm. Drain, rinse with cold water and drain again. Set aside. Heat 1 tablespoon oil in a skillet, add mushrooms and cook 2 to 3 minutes. Let cool; then place in a bowl with cooked pasta, olives, anchovies and oregano. Stir together 3 tablespoons oil and vinegar; pour over salad. Toss together; season with salt and pepper and serve.

Makes 4 to 6 servings.

PINE NUT, PASTA & FETA SALAD

1-2/3 cups pasta bows
6 bacon slices
1/2 cup (2 oz.) pine nuts
4 tomatoes, peeled, seeded and chopped
8 oz. feta cheese, cut into 1/2 inch cubes
2 tablespoons torn basil leaves

Dressing:
2 garlic cloves, crushed
2 tablespoons grated Parmesan cheese
2 tablespoons lemon or lime juice
1/4 cup virgin olive oil
1/2 teaspoon Dijon-style mustard
Salt and pepper, to taste

To Garnish:
Basil sprigs

Cook pasta in boiling salted water 10 minutes or until *al dente*; drain under cold water and set aside.

Meanwhile, in a skillet, cook bacon in its own fat until crispy; drain on paper towels, crumble and set aside. Remove all but 1 teaspoon of the bacon fat from skillet. Add pine nuts to pan and cook until golden. Remove from pan and set aside.

To make dressing, combine all ingredients in a jar with a lid and shake until well blended.

Put tomatoes and cheese into a salad bowl; add bacon, pine nuts and basil and mix thoroughly. Add dressing and mix again. Garnish with basil sprigs.

Makes 4 main-dish servings or 6 side-dish servings.

Note: This salad is best tossed in dressing about 20 minutes before serving, to allow flavors to develop.

GRAPE & GORGONZOLA SALAD

1/2 small melon
8 Romaine lettuce leaves
4 oz. seedless green grapes
3 oz. black grapes, seeded
3 oz. seedless red grapes

Dressing:
6 oz. Gorgonzola cheese, crumbled
3 tablespoons mayonnaise
1/4 cup chutney
1/4 teaspoon chili sauce
Squeeze of lemon juice

To Garnish:
Parsley sprigs
Few endive and radicchio leaves
A little paprika

First make dressing: combine all ingredients in a bowl; set aside. Cut melon into 4 slices; remove rind and seeds.

Place 2 lettuce leaves on each of 4 individual plates. Arrange melon and grapes among the leaves.

Put a spoonful of dressing on top of each salad and garnish with parsley, chicory and radicchio leaves. Sprinkle a little paprika over dressing just before serving.

Makes 4 servings.

Note: If a thinner dressing is desired, add half and half or milk until correct consistency is reached.

VINAIGRETTE DRESSING

1/4 teaspoon salt
1/2 teaspoon black pepper
1 teaspoon Dijon-style mustard
1 teaspoon superfine sugar
2/3 cup olive oil
2 tablespoons tarragon vinegar
2 tablespoons white wine vinegar

In a small bowl, whisk salt, pepper, mustard, sugar and olive oil until well blended. Whisk in tarragon and wine vinegar until cloudy and slightly thick. Cover with plastic wrap and refrigerate until needed.

Makes 2/3 cup.

Variations: To prepare *Herbed Dressing*, add 2 teaspoons snipped fresh chives, 2 teaspoons chopped fresh parsley, 2 teaspoons chopped fresh marjoram and 1 garlic clove crushed.

To prepare *Lemon Dressing*, substitute 2 teaspoons honey for sugar and lemon juice for tarragon vinegar. Add 2 teaspoons grated lemon peel and 1 tablespoon chopped fresh lemon verbena.

To prepare *Garlic Dressing*, add 2 crushed garlic cloves and 1 tablespoon chopped fresh parsley.

WALNUT DRESSING

1 teaspoon light-brown sugar
1 teaspoon Dijon-style mustard
1/4 teaspoon salt
1/2 teaspoon black pepper
1/2 cup walnut oil
2 tablespoons cider vinegar
1 tablespoon finely chopped walnuts
1 tablespoon chopped fresh sage

In a small bowl, whisk brown sugar, mustard, salt, pepper and walnut oil until well blended. Whisk in vinegar until cloudy and slightly thick. Cover with plastic wrap and refrigerate until needed. Just before using, stir in walnuts and sage.

Makes 2/3 cup.

Variations: Substitute peanut oil and peanuts, almond oil and almonds or hazelnut oil and hazelnuts for walnut oil and walnuts.

Note: Serve with a pasta salad and bell peppers.

BASIL & TOMATO MAYONNAISE

3 medium-size tomatoes
2 tablespoons plus 2 teaspoons fresh basil
1 garlic clove, crushed
1 tablespoon snipped fresh chives
1 teaspoon superfine sugar
2/3 cup mayonnaise
2 tablespoons plain yogurt

In a large bowl, cover tomatoes with boiling water. Let stand 1 minute. Peel tomatoes, cut in half and remove seeds. Finely chop tomatoes and basil. In a medium-size bowl, combine tomatoes, basil, garlic, chives and sugar with a wooden spoon. Stir in mayonnaise and yogurt until all ingredients are evenly blended. Cover with plastic wrap and refrigerate until needed.

Makes 1 cup.

Note: Use to coat pasta or rice salad or to toss cooked mixed vegetables. Serve as an accompaniment to lamb or chicken kebabs.

MAYONNAISE

2 large egg yolks
1/2 teaspoon Dijon-style mustard
1/2 teaspoon salt
1/4 teaspoon black pepper
1/4 teaspoon cayenne pepper
1-1/4 cups olive oil
1 teaspoon fresh lemon juice
6 to 8 teaspoons white wine vinegar
Boiling water, if needed

By Hand: Have all ingredients at room temperature. In a medium-size bowl, blend egg yolks, mustard, salt and peppers with a wooden spoon. Add olive oil drop by drop, beating well after each addition of oil. Beat thoroughly until mixture begins to thicken, then, beating constantly, slowly increase flow of oil to a steady stream. When all oil has been added, beat in lemon juice and enough vinegar to desired flavor. If needed, thin with boiling water. Cover and refrigerate until needed.

Makes 1-3/4 cups.

By Food Processor: In a food processor fitted with a metal blade, process egg yolks, mustard, salt and peppers until smooth. With processor running, add olive oil drop by drop until mixture begins to thicken. Increase flow to a steady stream until all oil is added. Add lemon juice and enough vinegar to give desired flavor. If needed, thin dressing with boiling water. Cover with plastic wrap and refrigerate until needed.

Makes 1-3/4 cups.

Variations: To prepare *Garlic Mayonnaise*, add 2 crushed garlic cloves to 2/3 cup mayonnaise.

To prepare *Herbed Mayonnaise*, add 1 teaspoon chopped fresh tarragon, chervil, marjoram, parsley or chives to 2/3 cup mayonnaise.

To prepare *Green Mayonnaise*, add 1/4 cup mixed chopped watercress, basil, and parsley to 2/3 cup mayonnaise.

PIZZAS & ITALIAN BREADS

If preferred, bake in a 14″ × 10″ jellyroll pan, or as 4 individual pizzas.

2-3/4 cups bread flour
1 teaspoon salt
1 teaspoon active dried yeast
1 teaspoon sugar
About 3/4 cup warm water (110F, 45C
1 tablespoon olive oil

Sift flour and salt into a medium bowl.

Herb or Nut Pizza Dough: Knead 2 table-spoons chopped fresh herbs (or 1 table-spoon dried herbs) into the dough. If preferred, knead 1 oz. chopped walnuts into the dough.

In a small bowl, combine yeast, sugar and 1/4 cup water; leave until frothy. Add yeast liquid to flour with remaining water and oil. Mix to a soft dough; knead on a floured surface 10 minutes until smooth. Place in a greased bowl; cover with plastic wrap. Let rise in a warm place 45 minutes or until doubled in size.

Whole-Wheat Pizza Dough: Use 2-1/4 cups whole-wheat flour and 1/4 cup wheat germ. Add extra water as required to form a soft dough.

Punch down dough and knead briefly. Oil a 12-inch pizza pan. Place dough in center of pan; press out to edges with your knuckles. Pinch up edges to make a rim. Use as directed in recipe.

Cornmeal Pizza Dough: Use 2-1/4 cups bread flour and 1/3 cup cornmeal.

PIZZA NAPOLITANA

1 recipe Traditional Pizza Dough, shaped
and ready for topping, page 40

Topping:
3 tablespoons olive oil
1 lb. tomatoes
1 garlic clove, crushed
Salt and pepper
8 oz. mozzarella cheese
1 (2 oz.) can anchovy fillets, drained
1 tablespoon chopped fresh oregano
Oregano leaves, to garnish

Preheat oven to 425F (220C). Brush
dough with 1 tablespoon oil. Place
tomatoes in a bowl. Pour enough boiling water over tomatoes to cover. Let
stand 1 minute. Drain, peel and coarsely chop. Spread over dough. Sprinkle
with garlic; season to taste with salt and
pepper.

Slice cheese thinly. Arrange over
tomatoes. Chop anchovies and sprinkle over cheese. Sprinkle with oregano
and remaining oil. Bake 20 minutes
until cheese has melted and dough is
crisp and golden. Garnish with oregano leaves. Serve at once.

Makes 4 servings.

PIZZA CARCIOFI

1 recipe Traditional Pizza Dough, shaped
and ready for topping, page 40

Topping:
2 tablespoons Tomato Topping, see left
1/2 cup (2 oz.) shredded Fontina cheese
1 (6 oz.) jar marinated artichoke hearts
8 sun-dried tomatoes in oil
Salt and pepper
Parsley leaves, to garnish

Preheat oven to 425F (220C). Spread
the dough with Tomato Topping.
Sprinkle with cheese.

Drain artichokes, reserving oil. Drain
tomatoes. Slice artichokes and arrange
over the cheese. Chop tomatoes
roughly and sprinkle over the artichokes. Season to taste with salt and
pepper. Sprinkle with 1 to 2 tablespoons of the reserved oil.

Bake 20 minutes until dough is golden.
Garnish with parsley.

Makes 4 servings.

PIZZA MARGHERITA

1 recipe Traditional Pizza Dough, page 40

Tomato Topping:
1 lb. tomatoes, peeled, page 41, or 1 (16 oz.) can tomatoes
2 tablespoons olive oil
1 onion, finely chopped
1 garlic clove, crushed
1 tablespoon tomato paste
1/2 teaspoon sugar
1 tablespoon chopped fresh basil
Salt and pepper

To Finish:
1 to 2 tablespoons olive oil
4 oz. mozzarella cheese
6 to 8 fresh basil leaves
Basil sprig, to garnish

Make Tomato Topping. Chop tomatoes, if using fresh. Heat oil in a medium saucepan. Add onion and garlic; cook until soft. Stir in tomatoes, tomato paste, sugar and basil. Season to taste with salt and pepper. Cover pan and simmer 30 minutes until thick.

Preheat oven to 425F (220C). Lightly grease a 12-inch pizza pan. Punch down dough and knead briefly. Place in prepared pan and press out to edges with your knuckles. Brush dough with 1 tablespoon oil. Spoon Tomato Topping over dough. Slice cheese thinly. Arrange over sauce. Sprinkle with salt and pepper to taste, 2 or 3 basil leaves and remaining oil. Bake 20 minutes until cheese has melted and dough is crisp and golden. Sprinkle with remaining basil leaves. Garnish with basil sprig. Serve at once.

Makes 4 servings.

PIZZA MARINARA

1 recipe Traditional Pizza Dough, shaped and ready for topping, page 40

Topping:
3 tablespoons olive oil
8 oz. tomatoes, peeled, page 41
3 large garlic cloves
Salt and pepper
Few capers, if desired

Preheat oven to 425F (220C). Brush dough with 1 tablespoon oil.

Quarter tomatoes and discard seeds. Chop coarsely and drain in a sieve. Spread over dough. Cut garlic into thick slices and sprinkle over tomatoes.

Season with salt and pepper. Sprinkle with remaining oil. Bake 20 minutes until dough is crisp and golden. Sprinkle with capers.

Makes 4 servings.

ITALIAN SAUSAGE PIZZA

1 recipe Traditional Pizza Dough, shaped
   and ready for topping, page 40

Topping:
2 tablespoons olive oil
1 recipe Tomato Topping, page 41
2 oz. mushrooms, finely sliced
3 spicy Italian sausages
2 tablespoons freshly grated Pecorino
   cheese
Salt and pepper
Grated Pecorino cheese and flat-leaf
   parsley, to garnish

Preheat oven to 425F (220C). Brush
dough with 1 tablespoon oil. Spread
Tomato Topping over dough and
sprinkle with mushrooms. With a
sharp knife, cut skins from the sausages
and discard. Cut meat into pieces and
arrange over mushrooms. Sprinkle
with 2 tablespoons grated cheese.
Season to taste with salt and pepper.

   Sprinkle remaining oil over top.
Bake 20 minutes until dough is crisp
and golden. Serve garnished with additional grated Pecorino cheese and flat-
leaf parsley.

Makes 4 servings.

FOUR SEASONS PIZZA

1 recipe Traditional Pizza Dough, made up
   to end of step 2, page 40

Topping:
3 tablespoons olive oil
2 oz. button mushrooms
2 oz. prosciutto (Parma ham)
6 pitted ripe olives
4 canned artichoke hearts, drained
2 oz. mozzarella cheese
1 tomato, peeled, page 41
Salt and pepper

Preheat oven to 425F (220C). Lightly
grease a baking sheet. Punch down
dough and knead briefly. Place dough
on baking sheet. Press out with your
knuckles to a 10-inch circle. Brush
dough with a little oil.

Heat 2 tablespoons oil in a medium
saucepan. Add mushrooms; cook 5
minutes. Mark dough into 4 equal
sections with a knife. Arrange mushrooms over one section. Cut ham in
strips and chop olives; sprinkle over
second section. Slice artichokes
thinly. Arrange over third section.
Slice cheese and tomato and arrange
over fourth section. Season to taste
with salt and pepper. Drizzle with
remaining oil. Bake 20 minutes until
dough is crisp and golden. Serve at
once.

Makes 4 servings.

Variation: Make this recipe as 4 individual pizzas, if preferred.

—PROSCIUTTO & OLIVE PIZZA—

1 recipe Traditional Pizza Dough, shaped
 and ready for topping, page 40

Topping:
6 oz. mozzarella cheese
4 slices prosciutto
2 tablespoons olive pulp, see note
2 tablespoons olive oil
Salt and pepper

To Garnish:
Prosciutto
Few olives
Basil sprigs

Preheat oven to 425F (220C). Make
the topping. Cut cheese and prosciutto
into cubes. Place in bowl with olive
pulp. Mix together and moisten with a
little oil if dry. Spread over dough.
Season to taste with salt and pepper
and sprinkle with remaining oil. Bake
20 minutes until dough is crisp and
golden. Garnish with curls of prosciutto, olives and basil sprigs.

Makes 4 servings.

Note: Olive pulp may be bought in jars
from gourmet shops.

—ROMAN PIZZA—

1 recipe Traditional Pizza Dough, made up
 to end of step 2, page 40

Topping:
3 tablespoons olive oil
2 large onions, chopped
1 lb. tomatoes, peeled, page 41, or 1 (16
 oz.) can tomatoes, drained, chopped
1 (6 oz.) can pimentos, drained
1 (2 oz.) can anchovy fillets
12 pitted ripe olives
Pimentos and olives, to garnish

Preheat oven to 425F (220C). Lightly
grease a 14″ × 10″ jellyroll pan. Punch
down dough and knead briefly. Place in
prepared pan; press out to edges with
your knuckles. Pinch up edges to make
a rim.

In a saucepan, heat 2 tablespoons
oil. Add onions; cook until soft. Chop
tomatoes, if fresh, add to pan and cook
2 minutes. Spoon over dough. Slice
pimentos in strips and arrange over
tomatoes. Drain anchovies, cut in half
lengthwise and arrange in a lattice
pattern on top. Halve olives and place
in gaps. Sprinkle with remaining oil.

Bake 20 minutes until dough is crisp
and golden. Garnish with pimento and
olives.

Makes 4 servings.

PIZZA WITH CLAMS

1 recipe Whole-Wheat Pizza Dough,
   shaped and ready for topping, page 40

Topping:
1 lb. clams in the shell or 1 (14 oz.) can
   clams
3 tablespoons olive oil
1 recipe Tomato Topping, page 41
Salt and pepper
Few drops hot pepper sauce
2 tablespoons chopped fresh parsley

Preheat oven to 425F (220C). If using clams in the shell, wash well and place in a saucepan with 1 tablespoon oil. Cover and cook over low heat until all the shells open. Discard any that do not open. Remove from heat; strain pan juices into a bowl. Reserve. Remove clams from their shells, reserving a few intact for garnishing. Place shelled clams in reserved juice.

Spread Tomato Topping over dough. Drizzle with remaining oil. Season to taste with salt and pepper and hot pepper sauce and 1 tablespoon chopped parsley. Bake 20 minutes until crust is crisp and golden. Spoon the shelled clams (or canned clams) and a little clam juice over pizza. Arrange reserved clams in shells on top. Sprinkle with remaining chopped parsley.

Makes 4 servings.

FOUR CHEESE PIZZA

1 recipe Traditional Pizza Dough, shaped
   and ready for topping, page 40

Topping:
2 tablespoons olive oil
2 oz. mozzarella cheese
2 oz. Gorgonzola cheese
2 oz. Fontina or Gruyère cheese
1/2 cup freshly grated Parmesan cheese
Salt and pepper
Chopped green onion and grated Parmesan
   cheese, to garnish

Preheat oven to 425F (220C). Brush dough with 1 tablespoon oil. Cut the first 3 cheeses into small cubes. Scatter over the dough. Sprinkle with Parmesan cheese; season to taste with salt and pepper. Drizzle with remaining oil.

Bake 20 minutes until cheese is melted and dough is crisp and golden. Garnish with green onion and additional Parmesan cheese.

Makes 4 servings.

CHICKEN LIVER CALZONE

1 recipe Traditional Pizza Dough, made to
end of step 2, page 40

Filling:
1/4 cup butter
1 lb. chicken livers, trimmed
6 bacon slices, chopped
1 tablespoon chopped fresh sage
1-1/2 lb. fresh spinach, trimmed
Salt and pepper
Lemon juice
Freshly grated nutmeg
Beaten egg, to glaze
Sage leaves, to garnish

Make the filling. In a medium saucepan, melt butter. Add livers; cook quickly until brown but still pink on the inside. Remove with slotted spoon and serve.

Add bacon to saucepan; cook until crisp. Remove with slotted spoon and add to livers with chopped sage. Add spinach to saucepan. Cover and cook until wilted. Drain well, then chop coarsely. Season to taste with salt and pepper, lemon juice and nutmeg.

Preheat oven to 425F (220C). Grease 2 baking sheets. Divide dough into 2 equal pieces. Roll out both pieces on a lightly floured surface to 10-inch circles. Brush lightly with oil.

Divide filling between the 2 dough pieces, confining it to one half of each circle. Dampen edges with water, then fold dough over to enclose filling and seal well by pressing with a fork. Transfer to baking sheets, brush with beaten egg and make 2 or 3 air holes with a sharp knife. Bake 20 minutes until golden.

Makes 4 to 6 servings.

MUSHROOM CALZONE

1 recipe Traditional Pizza Dough, made to
end of step 2, page 40

Filling:
1 lb. mushrooms, sliced
2 tablespoons olive oil
1 garlic clove, sliced
Salt and pepper
1/2 teaspoon dried leaf oregano
8 oz. ricotta cheese
**2 tablespoons freshly grated Parmesan
cheese**
Beaten egg, to glaze
**Grated Parmesan cheese and oregano
sprigs, to garnish**

Make the filling. In a medium saucepan, heat oil. Add mushrooms and garlic; cook 3 to 4 minutes. Remove with a slotted spoon and place in a bowl. Season to taste with salt and pepper; add oregano. Mix in ricotta cheese and 2 tablespoons Parmesan cheese.

Preheat oven to 425F (220C). Grease 2 baking sheets. Divide dough into 2 equal pieces. Roll out each piece on a lightly floured surface to a 10-inch circle. Brush lightly with oil.

Divide filling between the 2 dough pieces, confining it to one half of each circle. Dampen edges with water, then fold dough over to enclose filling and seal well by pressing with a fork. Transfer to baking sheets, brush with beaten egg and make 2 or 3 air holes with a sharp knife. Bake 20 minutes until golden. Garnish with grated Parmesan cheese and oregano sprigs.

Makes 4 to 6 servings.

HAM & SALAMI CALZONCELLI

1 recipe Traditional Pizza Dough, made up
  to end of step 2, page 40

Filling:
2 oz. sliced ham
2 oz. sliced salami
2 oz. mozzarella cheese
2 tablespoons chopped fresh parsley
1 tablespoon freshly grated Parmesan
  cheese
1 egg, beaten
Salt and pepper
Cress sprouts and radish slices, to garnish

Preheat oven to 425F (220C). Grease 2
baking sheets. Punch down dough and
knead briefly. Roll out. Using a 3 inch
cutter, cut out as many circles as pos-

sible, to make 10-15 in total.

Chop ham and salami very finely.
Place in a medium bowl. Shred mozzarella cheese. Add shredded cheese,
parsley and parmesan cheese to ham
mixture. Stir in egg and season to taste
with salt and pepper. Mix thoroughly.

Place 1 teaspoon of the mixture on
one half of each circle. Dampen edge
with water, then fold over to enclose
filling and seal well by pressing with a
fork. Transfer to baking sheets and
bake 15 minutes until golden. Garnish
with cress sprouts and radish slices.
Serve hot or cold.

Makes 10 to 15 servings.

BROCCOLI CALZONE

1 recipe Traditional Pizza Dough, made up
  to end of step 1, page 40
1 teaspoon dried dill weed
1 tablespoon olive oil

Filling:
12 oz. broccoli
2 cups (8 oz.) shredded Cheddar cheese
Salt and pepper
Beaten egg, to glaze
Chopped fresh dill, to garnish

In a medium saucepan of boiling water,
blanch broccoli 2 minutes. Drain and
refresh with cold water. Drain again.
Chop coarsely.

Preheat oven to 425F (220C).
Grease 2 baking sheets. Knead dough
with dill weed until evenly distributed.

Divide into 2 equal pieces. Roll out
each piece on a lightly floured surface
to a 10-inch circle. Brush lightly with
oil.

Divide broccoli between the 2 dough
pieces, confining it to one half of each
circle. Sprinkle with two-thirds of the
cheese and season with salt and pepper.
Dampen edges with water, fold dough
over to enclose filling and seal well by
pressing with a fork. Transfer to baking
sheets, brush with beaten egg and
sprinkle with remaining cheese. Make
2 or 3 air holes with a sharp knife. Bake
20 minutes until golden. Garnish with
fresh dill.

Makes 4 to 6 servings.

PANETTONE

2 (1/4 oz.) packages active dried yeast
1/3 cup warm water (110F, 45C)
1/3 cup sugar
4 egg yolks
1 teaspoon vanilla extract
Grated peel of 1 lemon
3 cups bread flour
1/2 teaspoon salt
1/3 cup butter, softened
1/3 cup chopped candied peel
2 tablespoons dark raisins
2 tablespoons golden raisins
1/4 cup butter, melted

In a small bowl, combine yeast, 1 teaspoon sugar and the water; leave until frothy.

In a large bowl, combine remaining sugar, egg yolks, vanilla and lemon peel. Stir in yeast mixture. Mix flour with salt. Gradually add two-thirds flour to yeast mixture to form a sticky dough.

Divide softened butter into 3 equal pieces. Add one piece at a time, kneading until mixture is heavy and stringy. Add remaining flour; mix well. Knead on a lightly floured surface until firm and buttery, but not sticky. Place in a bowl. Cover with plastic wrap; let rise in a warm place 1-1/2 hours until doubled.

Preheat oven to 400F (205C). Well grease a charlotte pan. Knead peel and raisins into dough. Place in pan, cover and let rise to just below top of pan.

Brush with melted butter; bake 10 minutes. Reduce temperature to 350F (175C). Brush again with butter; bake 30 to 40 minutes until browned. Brush with more butter after 15 minutes. Cool.

Makes 10 to 12 servings.

PIZZA LOAF

1 recipe Traditional Pizza Dough, made to
    end of step 1, page 40
3 oz. sliced salami, chopped
3 green onions, finely chopped
1 tablespoon chopped fresh herbs

Topping:
Melted butter for brushing
4 slices processed Cheddar cheese

Tomato & Basil Butter:
3/4 cup butter, softened
1 tablespoon tomato paste
2 tablespoons finely chopped basil
1 teaspoon lemon juice

Grease an 8″ × 4″ loaf pan. Punch down dough and knead dough with salami, green onions and herbs. Shape into a loaf. Cover with plastic wrap and let rise in a warm place until dough almost reaches top of pan.

Preheat oven to 375F (190C). Brush loaf with melted butter. Bake 25 to 30 minutes until loaf sounds hollow when bottom is tapped. Turn out of pan and place on a baking sheet. Slice cheese into strips and place in a lattice design over top. Return to oven 3 to 4 minutes to soften cheese a little. Cool.

Make Tomato & Basil Butter. In a small bowl, beat butter with tomato paste, basil and lemon juice. Spoon into a serving dish and cover and refrigerate until required. Slice Pizza Loaf and serve with Tomato & Basil Butter.

Makes 6 servings.

WALNUT BREAD

1 recipe Traditional Pizza Dough, made up
   to end of step 2, page 40
1-1/4 cups (5 oz.) chopped walnuts
Vegetable oil

Grease a baking sheet. Punch down
dough and knead in walnuts. Flatten to
a 10-inch round loaf shape. Place on
greased baking sheet. Cover with
plastic wrap and let rise in a warm place
1 to 1-1/2 hours until doubled in size.

Preheat oven to 375F (190C). Brush
dough with oil. With a sharp knife,
make 2 or 3 slashes across the top. Bake
20 to 25 minutes until bottom sounds
hollow when tapped. Cool on a wire
rack. Serve sliced and buttered with
cheese or plain with soup or pasta.

Makes 5 to 8 servings.

BREAD STICKS

1 recipe Traditional Pizza Dough, made up
   to end of step 2, page 40
Sesame or poppy seeds, or cracked wheat,
   to sprinkle

To Serve:
Slices of prosciutto, if desired

Preheat oven to 400F (200C). Grease
several baking sheets.

Punch down dough and knead
briefly. Divide dough into approxi-
mately 18 equal pieces and roll each
piece to an 8-inch length. Arrange on
greased baking sheets and brush with
water.

Leave plain or sprinkle with sesame
or poppy seeds, or cracked wheat, if
desired. Bake 15 to 20 minutes until
crisp and golden. Cool before serving
plain or wrapped with slices of prosciutto, if desired, to serve as a cocktail
snack.

Makes about 18.

POLENTA BREAD

1-1/3 cups coarse ground cornmeal
1 cup all-purpose flour
1-1/4 teaspoons salt
1/4 teaspoon pepper
3 tablespoons olive oil
1 cup lukewarm water

To Serve:
Salad

Preheat oven to 425F (220C). Grease a 12-inch pizza pan. In a medium bowl, mix together the cornmeal, flour, salt and pepper. In a small bowl, whisk together 2 tablespoons oil and water. Stir into the flour mixture with a fork to form a grainy paste.

Place in center of pan and press to edges with knuckles. Prick with a fork and brush with remaining oil. Bake 20 minutes until golden. Serve the bread warm with salad.

Makes 4 to 6 servings.

FOCACCIA

1 recipe Traditional Pizza Dough, made up
   to end of step 2, page 40
1 teaspoon crushed dried rosemary
About 18 pitted green olives
Coarse sea salt, to sprinkle
Rosemary sprigs, to garnish

Preheat oven to 425F (220C). Grease a 12-inch pizza pan.

Punch down dough and knead dough with crushed rosemary. Place dough in center of pan and press to edges with your knuckles. Prick all over with a fork. Press olives into dough. Brush with water and sprinkle with sea salt. Bake 20 minutes until crisp and golden. Garnish with rosemary.

Makes 4 to 6 servings.

Variations: Omit green olives and knead chopped ripe olives into dough with rosemary.

Or knead 1/2 cup freshly grated Parmesan cheese into dough and season to taste with a little pepper. In both cases, prick dough with a fork, brush with water and, if desired, sprinkle with sea salt before cooking.

PASTA

MAKING FRESH PASTA

BASIC PASTA DOUGH
2 eggs
1-1/2 cups bread flour
Pinch salt

Any quantity of pasta may be made by using the proportions of 1 egg to 3/4 cup flour, but the most convenient quantity to handle, particularly for a beginner, is a 2 to 3 egg mixture. Larger amounts should be mixed and rolled in batches.

Beat eggs in a large bowl. Sift flour and salt over eggs. Mix together with a fork, then press into a ball with the hands. It should be firm but pliable, and not sticky. Add more flour if too moist.

Turn the dough onto a lightly floured surface, and knead firmly 5 to 10 minutes or until smooth. Wrap in a damp towel and let rest 30 minutes at room temperate.

VARIATIONS

PASTA VERDI:
Cook 4 oz. spinach. Drain, squeeze out as much moisture as possible and chop very fine. Add spinach to the eggs and flour, adding extra flour if necessary.

TOMATO PASTA:
Add 1 tablespoon tomato paste to the eggs and flour.

HERB PASTA:
Add 1 tablespoon of a single fresh herb, such as parsley, or mixed fresh herbs, to the eggs and flour.

WHOLE-WHEAT PASTA:
Use whole-wheat flour in place of white flour or, for a lighter texture, a mixture of whole-wheat and white flour.

MASCARPONE & WALNUT SAUCE

1 tablespoon butter
1 cup mascarpone (8 oz.)
Milk as needed
3/4 cup walnuts, coarsely chopped (3 oz.)
1/4 cup shredded Parmesan cheese (3/4 oz.)

In a small saucepan, melt butter. Gradually stir in mascarpone. Cook over low heat, stirring, until sauce is smooth. If necessary, add a little milk to give a smooth, creamy consistency. Stir in walnuts and Parmesan cheese. Season with salt and pepper and serve at once.

Makes 4 servings.

Note: Serve over cooked spaghetti or tagliatelle.

CREAMY MUSHROOM & PEA SAUCE

1/3 cup butter
2 cups sliced mushrooms (4 oz.)
2/3 cup crème fraîche
2 egg yolks
1/2 cup grated Parmesan cheese (1-1/2 oz.)
Salt, pepper and nutmeg
1/2 (10 oz.) pkg. frozen green peas
Hot cooked pasta
Fresh mint, if desired

In a medium-size skillet, melt 2 tablespoons of butter. Add mushrooms. Cook gently until tender. Set aside. In a medium-size bowl, beat together crème fraîche, egg yolks, Parmesan cheese, salt, pepper and nutmeg. In a medium-size saucepan, melt remaining butter. Stir in crème fraîche mixture. Add peas. Cook over very low heat, stirring until mixture is heated through and begins to thicken slightly. Stir in cooked mushrooms. Serve over pasta at once and garnish with mint, if desired.

Makes 4 servings.

RABBIT SAUCE

1 (about 1 lb.) saddle of rabbit
1 cup dry red wine
1 onion, sliced
1 celery stalk, sliced
1 bay leaf
2 black peppercorns
2 tablespoons vegetable oil
6 bacon slices, chopped
1 onion, finely chopped
1 carrot, finely chopped
2 teaspoons all-purpose flour
2/3 cup chicken stock
Salt, pepper and nutmeg

Put rabbit in a medium-size bowl; cover with wine. Add sliced onion, celery, bay leaf and peppercorns. Cover bowl. Let marinate, in the refrigerator, 1 to 2 days. In a medium-size saucepan, heat oil. Add bacon, chopped onion and carrot. Cook gently until onion is soft. Remove rabbit from marinade; pat dry. Add to pan; brown all over. Stir in flour. Strain marinade; gradually add to pan with stock. Cover pan; cook over low heat 1-1/2 hours, or until rabbit is very tender. Remove rabbit from pan. Cut meat from bones. Chop into small pieces; return to pan.

Makes 4 servings.

Note: This sauce, is traditionally served with pappardells, a wide ribbon pasta.

CHICKEN LIVER SAUCE

2 tablespoons butter
4 bacon slices, chopped
1 medium-size onion, finely chopped
  (1/2 cup)
1 garlic clove, crushed
12 oz. chicken livers, chopped
  (1-1/2 cups)
2 teaspoons all-purpose flour
3/4 cup chicken stock
1 teaspoon tomato paste
Salt and pepper
1 teaspoon chopped fresh marjoram
1/4 cup dairy sour cream
Cooked rigatoni
Fresh marjoram, if desired

In a small saucepan, melt butter. Add bacon, onion and garlic. Cook over medium heat until onion is soft. Stir in chicken livers. Cook, stirring, until livers are no longer pink. Stir in flour. Gradually stir in stock. Add tomato paste, salt, pepper and chopped marjoram. Bring to a boil; reduce heat. Cover pan; simmer 10 minutes. Stir in sour cream and serve with rigatoni. Garnish with marjoram, if desired.

Makes about 3 cups sauce.

CARBONARA SAUCE

8 bacon slices
2 tablespoons butter
4 large eggs
1/2 cup grated Parmesan cheese
   (1-1/2 oz.)
2 tablespoons half and half
Salt and pepper
1 tablespoon chopped fresh chives
Cooked spaghetti or tagliatelle

Finely chop bacon. In a medium-size saucepan, melt butter over medium heat. Add bacon. Fry, stirring occasionally, until crisp. In a medium-size bowl, beat together eggs, Parmesan cheese, half and half, salt and pepper. Add to bacon. Cook over medium heat, stirring, until eggs begin to thicken. Stir in chives. Pour sauce over hot spaghetti or tagliatelle. Serve at once.

Makes 4 servings.

SHELLFISH SAUCE

1/3 cup olive oil
1 lb. fresh mussels in shells, cleaned
1 garlic clove, crushed
2 shallots, finely chopped
2/3 cup dry white wine
Salt and pepper
1 (8 oz.) can clams, drained
2 tablespoons chopped fresh parsley

In a deep skillet with a cover, heat 3 tablespoons of olive oil. Add mussels. Cover pan; cook over medium heat about 4 minutes until all mussels are open. Discard mussels that do not open. Heat remaining oil in a medium- size saucepan. Add garlic and shallots. Cook until shallots are soft. Drain mussels. Strain cooking liquid; add to shallots with white wine. Bring to a boil. Boil gently, uncovered, until reduced slightly. Season with salt and pepper. Remove most mussels from shells, leaving a few for garnishing. Add mussels and clams to cooking juice. Sprinkle parsley over sauce. Serve at once.

Makes 4 servings.

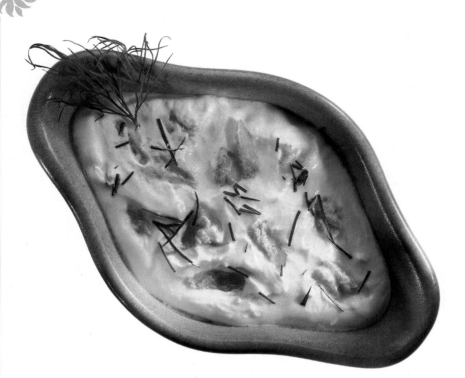

SALMON & CREAM SAUCE

2 tablespoons butter
1 pint half and half (2 cups)
1/4 cup grated Parmesan cheese (3/4 oz.)
2 cups cooked flaked salmon
1 tablespoon chopped fresh dill
Salt, pepper and nutmeg
Fresh dill, if desired

In a medium-size saucepan, heat butter and half and half over low heat. Bring to just below boiling point. Reduce heat. Simmer gently about 10 minutes or until thickened and slightly reduced. Add Parmesan cheese. Stir in salmon, chopped dill, salt, pepper and nutmeg. Garnish with dill, if desired.

Makes 4 servings.

PESTO

1/2 cup fresh basil leaves
1/2 cup pine nuts
2 garlic cloves
Salt
1/2 cup grated Parmesan cheese (1-1/2 oz.)
1/2 cup olive oil
Cooked pasta

Put basil leaves, pine nuts, garlic and salt in a blender or food processor. Process until mixture forms a paste. Add Parmesan cheese to basil mixture; process until well blended. Add oil, a little at a time; process until sauce has a creamy consistency.

Makes 4 to 6 servings.

Variation: When fresh basil leaves are unavailable, a version of pesto may be made with fresh parsley. Use walnuts instead of pine nuts.

Note: Pesto is used as a sauce for pasta, and is also added to dishes such as minestrone soup to give added flavor.

—SPAGHETTI WITH MEATBALLS—

1 bread slice, crusts removed
Water
1 onion, very finely chopped
1 garlic clove, crushed
1 lb. lean ground beef
1 tablespoon chopped fresh parsley
Salt and pepper
1 tablespoon vegetable oil
1 recipe Tomato Sauce, see right
12 oz. spaghetti
1/2 cup grated Parmesan cheese
  ·(1-1/2 oz.)
Fresh basil, if desired

Soak bread in a little water. Squeeze dry and crumble into a bowl. Add onion, garlic, ground beef, parsley, salt and pepper. Mix well. Shape in 1-inch balls. Heat oil in a 10-inch skillet over medium heat. Add meatballs. Cook about 10 minutes or until browned all over. Drain off excess fat. Add Tomato Sauce. Cook until heated through. Cook spaghetti until just tender to the bite. Drain well; pour into a heated serving dish. Add meatballs and sauce. Sprinkle with Parmesan cheese. Garnish with basil, if desired, and serve.

Makes 4 servings.

—TOMATO SAUCE—

1 lb. tomatoes (3 to 4 medium-size)
4 teaspoons olive oil
1 onion, finely chopped
1 garlic clove, crushed
1 tablespoon tomato paste
1/2 teaspoon sugar
1 tablespoon chopped fresh basil
Salt and pepper
Fresh basil, if desired

Put tomatoes in a medium-size bowl. Add boiling water to cover. Blanch 1 minute; drain. Peel; chop coarsely. In a medium-size saucepan, heat oil over medium heat. Add onion and garlic. Cook until soft. Stir in chopped tomatoes, tomato paste, sugar, chopped basil, salt and pepper. Cover pan; reduce heat to low and cook about 30 minutes or until thickened. If a thicker sauce is required, heat, uncovered, a few more minutes. Garnish with basil, if desired.

Makes 4 servings.

Note: For a smooth sauce, process in a blender or food processor.

——— BÉCHAMEL SAUCE ———

1-1/4 cups milk
1/2 bay leaf
1/4 cup butter
1/4 cup all-purpose flour
Salt and pepper

In a small saucepan, heat milk and bay leaf over low heat to just below boiling point. Remove from heat. Remove and discard bay leaf. In a small saucepan, melt butter over medium heat. Stir in flour, cook 2 minutes, stirring constantly. Remove from heat. Gradually stir in hot milk. Return pan to heat. Stir until thick and smooth. Reduce heat to low and cook 10 minutes stirring occasionally. Season with salt and pepper. If sauce is not to be used immediately, cover surface closely with plastic wrap.

Makes 4 servings.

Variation:
Ham & Mushroom Sauce
6 oz. fresh mushrooms, sliced (about 2-1/2 cups)
3 tablespoons dry apple cider
4 oz. ham, cut in shreds (about 1 cup)
Grated nutmeg
Béchamel Sauce made with 1-3/4 cups milk, 3 tablespoons each butter and all-purpose flour
Hot cooked pasta

In a small saucepan, combine mushrooms with cider. Cover pan. Cook over low heat 5 minutes. Add mushrooms, cooking liquid, ham and nutmeg to Béchamel Sauce. Serve with pasta.

— RICOTTA, LEEK & HAM SAUCE —

2 tablespoons butter
2 leeks, thinly sliced
1 garlic clove, crushed
4 (1 oz.) thin ham slices
8 oz. ricotta cheese (2 cups)
2/3 cup dairy sour cream
Milk
Pepper
Cooked tagliatelle

In a medium-size saucepan over medium heat, melt butter; add leeks and garlic. Cook until leeks are soft. Cut ham into small squares. Stir into leeks. Cook a few minutes. In a medium-size bowl, mix together ricotta and sour cream. Add a little milk, if necessary, to make a smooth creamy sauce. Season with pepper. Add to pan with leeks and ham. Reduce heat to low; cook until sauce is heated through. Serve at once with tagliatelle.

Makes 4 servings.

GREEN & BLUE SAUCE

8 oz. broccoli
6 oz. Gorgonzola cheese
1/2 cup mascarpone (3-1/2 oz.)
1 cup plain yogurt
Pepper

Wash and trim broccoli, discarding stalks. Cut in small flowerets. Cook in boiling salted water 2 to 3 minutes or until crisp-tender. Drain thoroughly. Roughly chop cheese. Put cheese and mascarpone in a small saucepan. Stir over low heat until cheese has melted. Add broccoli and yogurt to cheese sauce. Heat gently, stirring occasionally, 2 minutes.

Makes 4 servings.

BOLOGNESE SAUCE

2 tablespoons vegetable oil
2 slices bacon, chopped
1 onion, finely chopped
1 carrot, finely chopped
1 celery stalk, finely chopped
1 garlic clove, crushed
8 oz. lean ground beef
4 oz. chicken livers, chopped (1/2 cup)
2 tablespoons tomato paste
1/2 cup dry white wine
1/2 cup beef stock
Salt, pepper and nutmeg
Hot cooked spaghetti
Celery leaves, if desired

In a large saucepan, heat oil over medium heat. Add bacon; cook until lightly browned. Add onion, carrot, chopped celery and garlic to bacon. Cook, stirring occasionally, until beginning to brown. Add ground beef; cook, stirring occasionally, until evenly browned. Stir in chicken livers; cook until they are no longer pink. Drain off excess fat. Stir in tomato paste, wine, stock and seasonings. Cover and bring to a boil. Cook over low heat 30 to 40 minutes. Serve with spaghetti. Garnish with celery leaves, if desired.

Makes about 3 cups.

— CANNELLONI AU GRATIN —

1/4 cup butter
1 medium-size onion, finely chopped
1 garlic clove, crushed
6 cups sliced mushrooms (12 oz.)
1 tablespoon all-purpose flour
3/4 cup crème fraîche
Salt, pepper and nutmeg
Herb Pasta using 1 egg, see page 52
6 very thin prosciutto slices
1/2 cup fresh bread crumbs
1/4 cup grated Parmesan cheese (3/4 oz.)
Additional proscuitto slice, if desired
Fresh mint, if desired

In a medium-size saucepan over low heat, melt butter. Add onion and garlic; cook until soft. Add mushrooms; cook, stirring, until soft and most of liquid has evaporated. Stir in flour; add 1/3 cup of crème fraîche to form a thick sauce. Season with salt, pepper and nutmeg. Preheat oven to 350F (175C). Roll out pasta; cut out 6 (5" × 4") rectangles. Put a prosciutto slice on each rectangle, spoon some mushroom filling across each 1 and roll up from short end. Pack tightly, seams down, in a greased 1-1/2 quart oblong baking dish. Pour remaining crème fraîche over top and sprinkle with mixed bread crumbs and Parmesan cheese. Bake 20 minutes or until golden and bubbling. Garnish with additional proscuitto slice and mint, if desired.

Makes 6 first-course servings.

RAVIOLI WITH BUTTER & SAGE

1/3 cup butter
1 medium-size onion, chopped
8 oz. ground pork
8 oz. ground veal
2 tablespoons tomato paste, dissolved in 1/4 cup water
Salt, pepper and nutmeg
1/2 cup fresh bread crumbs
2 egg yolks
1 cup grated Parmesan cheese (3 oz.)
Fresh Pasta, using 3 eggs, see page 52
Fresh sage leaves

To make filling, in a medium-size saucepan, melt 2 tablespoons of butter; add onion and cook until soft. Add meat; cook, stirring until brown. Stir in tomato paste mixture and season with salt, pepper and nutmeg. Cover and simmer 30 minutes. Cool, then process in a blender or food processor until smooth, adding bread crumbs, egg yolks and cheese. Make ravioli; see page 61, filling with meat mixture. Drop ravioli into boiling salted water and cook 15 to 20 minutes or until tender but firm. Drain and place in a heated serving dish. Melt remaining butter, pour over ravioli. Season with pepper and garnish with sage leaves. Serve at once.

Makes 6 first-course servings.

MAKING FILLED PASTA

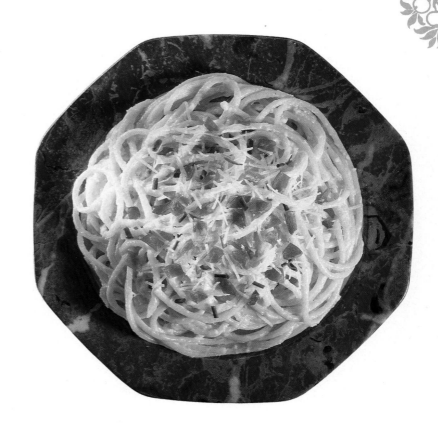

RAVIOLI:
When making ravioli, prepare the filling first and set aside. Then make the dough, see page 52, and roll into strips. Lay the strips out on a towel or floured surface and keep those you are not working on covered with a damp cloth.

Place small amounts (1/2 teaspoon) filling at 1-1/2 inch intervals over sheet of pasta and lay a second sheet over the top.

BUCATINI WITH FOUR CHEESES

6 oz. bucatini
1-1/4 cups half and half
1/2 cup grated Parmesan cheese
   (1-1/2 oz.)
3 oz. Gruyère cheese, cut into small dice
3 oz. soft goat's cheese
3 oz. mozzarella cheese, cut into small dice
Pepper
Chopped ham, if desired
Chopped chives, if desired

Press down firmly between the mounds of pasta, and cut between the mounds with a pastry wheel. Spread the ravioli out on a towel to dry about 30 minutes, turning over after 15 minutes. Take care to keep separate, or they will stick together. Round ravioli, or agnolotti, is made by cutting circles from the filled sheets of pasta.

In a large saucepan of boiling salted water, cook bucatini until just tender to the bite. Drain bucatini. Put half and half in a large saucepan with half of Parmesan cheese. Add Gruyère cheese, goat's cheese and mozzarella cheese. Cook over low heat until cheeses are melted. Season with pepper. Add drained bucatini to cheese mixture. Stir well. Sprinkle with remaining Parmesan cheese, ham and chives, if desired. Serve at once.

Makes 4 servings

VERMICELLI TIMBAL

4 oz. fine vermicelli
1/2 recipe Béchamel Sauce, see page 58
4 oz. mozzarella cheese
4 oz. ham
1 tablespoon butter
1/4 cup fresh bread crumbs
1 recipe Tomato Sauce, see page 57
Fresh mint, if desired

In a large saucepan of boiling salted water, cook vermicelli until just tender to the bite. Drain. In a medium-size bowl, combine drained vermicelli and Béchamel Sauce. Set aside. Preheat oven to 425F (220C). Butter 6 (6 oz.) custard cups. Coat with 1/2 of bread crumbs. Cut cheese and ham in small dice. Half fill each custard cup with pasta mixture. Divide cheese and ham among cups. Fill cups with pasta mixture. Sprinkle tops with remaining bread crumbs. Bake 15 minutes or until bubbly. Run a sharp knife around inside of cups. Turn out onto warmed serving plates. Serve with Tomato Sauce. Garnish with mint, if desired.

Makes 6 servings.

LASAGNE

8 oz. lasagne noodles
1 recipe Béchamel Sauce, see page 58
4 oz. mozzarella cheese, cubed
1 recipe Bolognese Sauce, see page 59
2 tablespoons grated Parmesan cheese
Zucchini slices, if desired
Shredded radicchio, if desired
Endive leaves, if desired

In a large saucepan of boiling salted water, cook noodles, in 2 batches, about 10 minutes or until just tender to the bite. Drain thoroughly. Spread out on paper towels. Preheat oven to 350F (175C). In a saucepan, heat Béchamel Sauce. Add mozzarella cheese; stir until melted. Arrange a noodle layer in bottom of a greased 3 quart oblong baking dish. Spoon half of Bolognese Sauce over top. Cover with noodles. Spread with half of cheese sauce. Repeat layers finishing with remaining cheese sauce. Sprinkle with Parmesan cheese. Bake 30 to 40 minutes or until bubbly. Garnish with zucchini slices, radicchio and endive leaves, if desired, and serve.

Makes 4 to 6 servings.

PEPPER GRATIN

2 large red bell peppers
2 large yellow bell peppers
1/2 cup olive oil
1 garlic clove, crushed
4 anchovy fillets, drained, chopped
8 pitted ripe olives, chopped
1 tablespoon capers
Salt and pepper
8 oz. spaghetti
2 tablespoons fresh bread crumbs
2 tablespoons grated Parmesan cheese
Green bell pepper strips, if desired
Additional ripe olives, if desired

Cook bell peppers under broiler. Turn peppers at intervals until skins are blistered and blackened. Cool in a paper bag. Preheat oven to 375F (190C). Scrape off skins of bell peppers; cut in strips. In a 10-inch skillet, beat 1/4 cup of olive oil. Add cooked bell pepper strips and garlic. Cook 2 to 3 minutes or until softened. Stir in anchovies, chopped olives and capers. Season with salt and pepper. In a large saucepan of boiling salted water, cook spaghetti until just tender to the bite. Drain and return to pan. Toss with 2 tablespoons of remaining olive oil. Combine bread crumbs and Parmesan cheese; sprinkle half of mixture over bottom of a 2 quart oblong baking dish. Spoon half of bell-pepper mixture over bread-crumb mixture. Cover with cooked spaghetti. Spoon remaining bell-pepper mixture over spaghetti, then sprinkle with remaining bread-crumb mixture. Drizzle with remaining 2 tablespoons of olive oil. Bake 20 minutes or until golden brown. Garnish with bell pepper strips and additional olives, if desired.

Makes 4 servings.

BAKED COD ITALIENNE

2 tablespoons butter
2 cups sliced mushrooms (4 oz.)
1 recipe Tomato Sauce, see page 57
4 (4 to 5 oz.) white fish steaks, such as cod
Salt and pepper
1 cup pasta shells (4 oz.)
8 ripe olives

Preheat oven to 375F (190C). In a medium-size saucepan, melt butter. Add mushrooms; cook gently until soft. Stir in Tomato Sauce. Put fish into a buttered 2 quart oblong baking dish. Season with salt and pepper. Pour tomato and mushroom sauce over fish. Cover dish with foil; bake about 25 minutes or until fish is opaque when tested with a fork. Meanwhile, cook pasta until just tender to the bite. About 5 minutes before fish has finished cooking, arrange pasta around fish, spooning some of sauce over pasta. Garnish with olives and serve.

Makes 4 servings.

VEGETARIAN BOLOGNESE SAUCE ——— TURKEY TETRAZZINI

2-3/4 cups water
1 cup lentils (6 oz.)
2/3 cup split peas (4 oz.)
2 tablespoons vegetable oil
1 onion, finely chopped
1 garlic clove, crushed
1 carrot, finely chopped
1 celery stalk, finely chopped
1 (15 oz.) can tomatoes, drained, chopped
1 teaspoon dried leaf oregano
Salt and pepper

In a medium-size saucepan, bring water to a boil. Stir in lentils and split peas. Simmer, covered, about 40 minutes or until all liquid has been absorbed and lentils and peas are soft. In a medium-size saucepan, heat oil. Add onion, garlic, carrot and celery. Cook over low heat, stirring occasionally, until soft. Stir in tomatoes and oregano. Season with salt and pepper. Cover pan; simmer gently 5 minutes. Add cooked lentils and split peas to vegetable mixture. Cook, stirring occasionally, until well combined and heated through.

Makes 4 to 6 servings

Note: Serve with whole-wheat spaghetti, if desired.

1/4 cup butter
4 (1 oz.) thin ham slices, chopped
1 onion, finely chopped
2 cups sliced mushrooms (4 oz.)
1/3 cup all-purpose flour
1-3/4 cups chicken stock
2/3 cup whipping cream
2 tablespoons dry sherry
2 cups cubed cooked turkey
8 oz. red, green and white tagliatelle, cooked
Salt, pepper and nutmeg
1/4 cup grated Parmesan cheese (3/4 oz.)
Fresh parsley, if desired

Preheat oven to 350F (175C). In a medium-size saucepan, melt butter over medium heat. Add ham and onion. Cook until onion is soft. Add mushrooms; cook until soft. Stir in flour; cook, stirring constantly, 2 minutes. Gradually stir in stock. Simmer, stirring constantly, until sauce is thickened and smooth. Remove pan from heat. Stir in whipping cream, sherry, turkey and tagliatelle. Season with salt, pepper and nutmeg. Pour into a greased 2-quart baking dish. Sprinkle with Parmesan cheese. Bake 30 minutes or until golden brown. Garnish with parsley, if desired.

Makes 4 servings.

PASTA WITH SPINACH & RICOTTA

1 lb. spinach
2 cups ricotta cheese (8 oz.)
1/2 cup grated Parmesan cheese
    (1-1/2 oz.)
1 egg yolk
Salt, pepper and nutmeg
Fresh Pasta, using 3 eggs, see page 52
1/3 cup butter
2 tablespoons chopped fresh mixed herbs
    (about 1/2 teaspoon dried mixed herbs)
2 teaspoons lemon juice

In a large saucepan, cook spinach in a small amount of water until tender. Drain; cool. Squeeze spinach dry; chop in a blender or food processor. Add ricotta cheese, Parmesan cheese, egg yolk, salt, pepper and nutmeg. Process

until fairly smooth. Roll out pasta. Cut in 2 inch squares. Put 1/2 teaspoon of filling in middle of each square. Fold in half to make a triangle; press edges to seal. Wrap long side of triangle around index finger; press ends together. Leave on a towel to dry, turning after 1 hour. Cook cappelletti in a large saucepan of boiling water 10 to 15 minutes or until tender but firm. In a small saucepan, melt butter; stir in herbs and lemon juice. Drain cappelletti; put into a heated serving dish. Add herb butter sauce; stir thoroughly. Serve at once.

Makes 6 first-course servings, 4 main-course servings.

VEGETARIAN LASAGNE

1 cup adzuki beans (6 oz.), soaked
    overnight
4 cups cold water
6 to 8 whole-wheat lasagne noodles
2 tablespoons vegetable oil
1 onion, finely chopped
1 garlic clove, crushed
8 oz. white cabbage, coarsely shredded
    (4 cups)
2 cups sliced mushrooms (4 oz.)
1 leek, coarsely chopped
1/2 green bell pepper, coarsely chopped
1 (15 oz.) can tomatoes
1 teaspoon dried leaf oregano
Salt and pepper
1 recipe Béchamel Sauce, see page 58,
    made with whole-wheat flour
1/2 cup shredded Cheddar cheese (2 oz.)
Fresh tarragon, if desired

Drain adzuki beans. Put into a saucepan with cold water. Bring to a boil. Cover pan; reduce heat. Simmer 40 minutes or until tender. Cook noodles

until tender to the bite. Drain; lay on paper towels. In a large saucepan, heat oil. Add onion and garlic. Cook until soft. Stir in cabbage, mushrooms, leek and bell pepper. Cook 5 minutes, stirring occasionally. Drain adzuki beans, reserving cooking liquid. Add beans to vegetables. Stir in tomatoes with juice and 1 cup of cooking liquid from beans. Add oregano. Season with salt and pepper. Cover pan; simmer gently 30 minutes, stirring occasionally. Preheat oven to 350F (175C). In a greased baking dish, layer noodles, vegetables and Béchamel sauce, ending with a layer of sauce. Sprinkle cheese over top. Bake 30 minutes or until golden and bubbling. Garnish with tarragon, if desired.

Makes 4 to 6 servings.

Note: Serve with a carrot salad.

SPINACH & HAM CANNELLONI

1 lb. fresh spinach
2 tablespoons butter
1 medium-size onion, finely chopped
1 tablespoon all-purpose flour
2/3 cup milk
4 oz. ham, finely chopped (1/2 cup)
Salt, pepper and nutmeg
8 ready-to-use cannelloni tubes
1 recipe Béchamel Sauce, see page 58
3/4 cup grated Cheddar cheese (3 oz.)
2 (1 oz.) ham slices, cut in strips, if desired
Fresh bay leaves, if desired

In a medium-size covered saucepan, cook spinach in a little water until tender. Drain thoroughly. Chop until fine. In the same saucepan over medium heat, melt butter. Add onion and cook until soft. Stir in flour and cook 1 minute. Gradually stir in milk; boil 1 minute. Stir in spinach, chopped ham, salt, pepper and nutmeg. Using a teaspoon, push spinach mixture into cannelloni tubes. Preheat oven to 425F (220C). In a small saucepan, heat Béchamel Sauce over low heat. Stir in 1/2 cup of the cheese. Pour 1/2 of the sauce into a greased oblong 1 quart baking dish. Arrange cannelloni in a single layer in dish; pour remaining sauce over top. Bake 40 minutes or until golden and bubbling. Arrange ham strips in a lattice pattern on top, if desired, and sprinkle with remaining cheese. Garnish with bay leaves, if desired.

Makes 4 servings.

DEEP-FRIED RAVIOLI

1 (10 oz.) pkg. frozen chopped spinach, cooked, drained
1-1/3 cups chopped cooked chicken
2 egg yolks
1/3 cup grated Parmesan cheese (1 oz.)
Salt, pepper and nutmeg
Fresh Pasta, using 3 eggs, see page 52
Vegetable oil for deep-frying
Lemon and lime slices, if desired
Fresh parsley, if desired

Squeeze as much water as possible from spinach. In a blender or food processor, process spinach, chicken, egg yolks and Parmesan cheese until quite smooth. Season with salt, pepper and nutmeg. Roll out pasta dough. Using chicken mixture as a filling, make ravioli, see page 61. In a deep fryer, heat oil to 375F (190C) or until a 1 inch bread cube turns golden in 40 seconds. Fry ravioli in batches until crisp and golden brown. Drain on paper towels. Garnish with lemon and lime slices and parsley, if desired, and serve.

Makes 4 servings.

SNACKS & SIDE DISHES

— SALAMI & MELON SNACK —

4 slices pumpernickel bread
2 tablespoons butter, softened
12 thin slices salami
1/2 small melon
1 tablespoon mayonnaise
1 tablespoon dairy sour cream
1 teaspoon capers, chopped
1/2 teaspoon pink peppercorns, crushed

Spread bread with butter and arrange 3 salami slices on each. Remove seeds and peel melon; slice thinly in 12 pieces. Arrange 3 slices on each sandwich. In a small bowl, mix mayonnaise and sour cream and spoon onto melon. Sprinkle with capers and peppercorns.

Makes 4 servings.

— SOUFFLÉ-FILLED TOMATOES —

4 medium-size tomatoes
Salt and pepper, to taste
4 (1-inch-thick) slices white bread
1/3 cup garlic-herb butter, see note
1 (6 oz.) can tuna, drained
2 tablespoons fresh bread crumbs
1 teaspoon pesto sauce
1 egg, separated
1 teaspoon grated Parmesan cheese
Sprigs of basil to garnish

Cut tops off tomatoes and remove seeds and pulp. Reserve tomato pulp for another use. Season insides of tomatoes with salt and pepper. Turn upside down on paper towels to drain. Remove crusts from bread, and using a 2-inch cookie cutter, cut holes in center of each slice. Prepare 2 tablespoons of bread crumbs from bread holes. In a small saucepan, melt 1/4 cup of garlic-herb butter and brush over both sides of each slice of bread. Place bread on a baking sheet and set aside. Preheat oven to 400F (205C). In a small saucepan, melt remaining butter and stir in bread crumbs, tuna and pesto sauce. In a small bowl, whisk egg white until stiff. Stir egg yolk into tuna mixture and fold in egg white. Set tomatoes in holes in bread and fill with tuna mixture. Sprinkle with Parmesan cheese and bake in preheated oven 12 to 15 minutes, until soufflé is well risen and golden and bread is crisp. Garnish with sprigs of basil and serve immediately.

Makes 4 servings

Note: To prepare garlic-herb butter, flavor 1/3 cup softened butter with crushed garlic and chopped fresh herbs to taste.

NEAPOLITAN CREPES

7-inch crepes

2 tablespoons butter
1 tablespoon olive oil
1 lb. onions, thinly sliced
1 (14 oz.) can tomatoes
1 (3 oz.) can anchovies, drained and chopped
3 tablespoons tomato puree
8 pimiento-stuffed olives, sliced
1 teaspoon chopped fresh basil
Salt and pepper
4 pimiento-stuffed olives, halved
Basil leaves

Keep crepes warm while preparing filling. Combine butter and oil in a medium-size saucepan over low heat. Add onions and cook 5 minutes. Add undrained tomatoes, anchovies, tomato puree, sliced olives, basil, salt and pepper. Cover and simmer 30 minutes, stirring occasionally.

Preheat oven to 350F (175C). Divide filling between crepes. Roll up and arrange in single layer in shallow heatproof dish. Cover with foil. Bake 20 minutes. Garnish with olives and basil.

Serves 4.

MOZZARELLA & CROUTON CREPES

7-inch crepes

1/4 cup butter
1 (1-inch) thick slice bread, cubed
1 cup (4 oz.) diced Mozzarella cheese
Salt and pepper
1/3 cup grated Parmesan cheese
Basil sprigs

Keep crepes warm while preparing filling. Heat butter in a small skillet over medium heat. Add bread cubes and cook, stirring often, until golden. Remove from heat and stir in Mozzarella. Season with salt and pepper.

Preheat broiler. Divide filling between crepes. Roll up and arrange in a single layer in a shallow heatproof dish. Sprinkle with Parmesan. Broil until lightly browned, about 2 minutes. Garnish with sprigs of basil.

Serves 4.

ITALIAN OMELET

Filling:
4 tablespoons butter
1 small onion, finely chopped
1 medium-size tomato, peeled and chopped
1 tablespoon chopped green pepper

Omelet:
3 eggs
2 oz. (1/3 cup) cooked pasta
Salt and pepper
2 tablespoons grated Parmesan cheese
Basil leaves

Prepare filling before making omelet. Melt 2 tablespoons butter in a small saucepan over low heat. Add onion and cook, stirring occasionally, 2 minutes. Stir in tomato and green pepper. Cover and cook 10 minutes.

Preheat broiler. In a small bowl, beat eggs until just mixed. Stir in pasta. Season with salt and pepper. Set 7-inch omelet pan over low heat to become thoroughly hot. Add remaining butter to pan. When butter is sizzling but not brown, pour in egg mixture. Using a fork or spatula, draw mixture from sides to middle of pan, allowing uncooked egg to run underneath. Repeat two or three times until egg rises slightly and becomes fluffy. Cook until golden-brown underneath and top is slightly runny, about 2 minutes.

Spread filling over half the omelet. Fold over and sprinkle with Parmesan. Broil just long enough to melt cheese, about 30 seconds. To serve, cut in half and garnish with basil.

Serves 2.

FLORENTINE OMELET

4 oz. fresh spinach, well-washed
1/2 recipe cheese sauce
Basic Omelet (see left)
1/2 cup (2 oz.) shredded Cheddar cheese
Cayenne pepper

Prepare filling before making omelet. Cook spinach in a small saucepan over low heat until very tender. Drain well; press out excess moisture. Warm Cheese Sauce.

Preheat broiler. Make omelet. Spoon spinach over half the omelet. Fold over and lift onto a warm heat-proof plate. For the sauce, follow basic method on page 73 and add 1/2 cup grated Cheddar cheese. Keep warm. Spoon cheese sauce over top; sprinkle with cheese and cayenne. Broil until sauce is bubbling and lightly browned.

Serves 1.

PROSCIUTTO & SAGE CRESPELLINI

4 slices prosciutto, cut in half
8 large sage leaves
2 eggs
3/4 cup all-purpose flour
Pinch salt
1/3 cup milk
Vegetable oil for frying

Wine Sauce:
1/4 cup butter
1 tablespoon all-purpose flour
1/3 cup white wine
Salt and pepper to taste
4 teaspoons whipping cream
3 tablespoons grated Parmesan cheese

Tomato Sauce:
2 teaspoons olive oil
8 oz. tomatoes, skinned, seeded, chopped
1 garlic clove, crushed
salt and pepper to taste

To make crespellini, mix eggs, flour, salt and milk in a blender or food processor. Chill 1 to 2 hours.

Heat oil in a crepe pan. Using 2 tablespoons batter, tilt pan to spread batter. Cook on both sides. Makes 8 crespellini.

To make wine sauce, melt butter. Add flour and cook, stirring, 1 to 2 minutes to form a roux. Add warm wine, stirring. Season and simmer 20 minutes, stirring occasionally. Remove from heat and stir in cream and Parmesan.

Meanwhile, prepare tomato sauce. Heat oil and add remaining ingredients. Simmer 15 to 20 minutes.

Preheat oven to 350F (175C). Cover bottom of a baking dish with a thin layer of wine sauce. Place a half slice of prosciutto, a sage leaf and 2 teaspoons tomato sauce on each crespellini. Fold over and place in baking dish. Pour over remaining wine sauce and bake 15 minutes.

Makes 4 servings.

VEGETABLES WITH RICOTTA

6 tomatoes
6 small zucchini
1/2 cup ricotta cheese
1/4 cup sour cream
1 teaspoon chopped lemon thyme
1 teaspoon chopped marjoram
Salt and black pepper to taste
2 tablespoons chopped green pitted olives
3 to 4 tablespoons chopped pistachio nuts
2 teaspoons dried bread crumbs
2 tablespoons olive oil

To Garnish:
Lemon thyme sprigs
Marjoram sprigs

Preheat oven to 350F (175C).

Cut tops off tomatoes. Scoop out flesh and invert tomatoes to drain. Cut zucchini in half lengthwise and scoop out flesh.

Sieve ricotta cheese into a bowl; mix in sour cream, thyme, marjoram and season with salt and pepper.

Fill tomatoes 3/4 full with ricotta mixture; top with chopped olives. Fill zucchini with ricotta mixture. Top with pistachio nuts, then bread crumbs.

Place vegetables in an ovenproof dish large enough to hold them in 1 layer. Drizzle olive oil over them. Put a little water in bottom of dish and bake, uncovered, in a oven 20 to 25 minutes, until zucchini are tender.

Transfer vegetables to a serving dish and garnish with lemon thyme and marjoram sprigs. Serve hot.

Makes 6 servings.

—ITALIAN COUNTRY FRITTATA—

4 tablespoons vegetable oil
1 medium-size zucchini, diced
1 celery stalk, diced
2 medium-size tomatoes, peeled, seeded
    and chopped
Salt and pepper
4 eggs
2 tablespoons grated Parmesan cheese
1 teaspoon chopped fresh basil
Extra Parmesan cheese for sprinkling
Mint sprigs

Heat 2 tablespoons oil in a large skillet over low heat. Add zucchini and celery and cook gently 5 minutes. Add tomatoes, salt and pepper and simmer, stirring occasionally, for 15 minutes.

In a small bowl, beat eggs with cheese and basil. Add remaining oil to pan and heat 1 minute. Pour in egg mixture and cook 4 minutes. Carefully flip mixture and continue cooking second side 4 minutes. Cut into quarters and sprinkle with Parmesan. Garnish with mint sprigs and serve immediately.

Serves 4.

—FISH CRESPOLINI—

7-inch crepes

3/4 lb. white fish fillets
2 cups milk
2 tablespoons butter
2 tablespoons all-purpose flour
4 medium-size tomatoes, peeled, seeded
    and chopped
1 tablespoon lemon juice
Salt and pepper
3/4 cup (3 oz.) shredded Cheddar cheese
Watercress sprigs and sliced cherry
    tomatoes

Keep crepes warm while preparing filling. Arrange fish in a medium-size skillet; cover with half the milk. Poach until fish is just cooked through. Remove fish with slotted spoon; reserve poaching liquid. Flake fish and set aside. Melt butter in a small saucepan over low heat. Stir in flour and cook 30 seconds. Remove from heat and stir in reserved liquid and remaining milk. Return to low heat and cook, stirring constantly, until sauce is thick and smooth. Divide sauce in half.

Preheat oven to 375F (190C). Stir fish, tomatoes and lemon juice into half the sauce; season with salt and pepper. Divide between crepes. Roll up and arrange in single layer in shallow heatproof dish. Stir cheese into remaining sauce and spoon over crepes. Bake until sauce is bubbling, about 20 minutes. Garnish with watercress and tomatoes.

Serves 4.

ASPARAGUS GRATIN

1-1/2 lbs. asparagus

Sauce:
1 leek, finely chopped
2 teaspoons all-purpose flour
3/4 cup milk
4 teaspoons chopped tarragon
2 tablespoons whipping cream
Salt and black pepper to taste
1 egg

To Garnish:
Tarragon sprigs

Preheat oven to 375F (190C).

Trim and cook asparagus in usual way; drain off cooking water, reserving 1/3 cup. Set asparagus aside.

To prepare sauce, in a saucepan, melt 1/2 of butter. Add leek, cover and cook gently 5 minutes.

Stir in flour and cook gently 2 to 3 minutes.

In a separate pan, heat milk and reserved asparagus cooking liquid; do not allow to boil. Add to roux and stir over low heat until sauce has thickened. Remove from heat and stir in tarragon, cream and season with salt and pepper. Beat egg lightly and stir into sauce.

Lay asparagus in a gratin dish, tips facing alternate ends. Pour over sauce, dot with remaining butter and bake in oven 10 to 12 minutes, until golden and sauce is bubbling.

Serve from baking dish, garnished with tarragon sprigs.

Makes 4 to 6 servings.

POTATOES & ROSEMARY

2 lbs. potatoes
1/4 cup butter
2 onions, thinly sliced
1 (1-3/4-oz.) can anchovy fillets, drained, chopped
2 garlic cloves, crushed
About 5 teaspoons finely chopped rosemary
Salt and black pepper to taste
1 cup milk

To Garnish:
Rosemary sprigs

Slice potatoes thinly and place in a bowl of cold water until ready to use. Preheat oven to 400F (205C).

In a skillet, melt 1/2 of butter. Fry onions a few minutes until softened; set aside.

Butter a gratin dish. Drain potato slices and dry on paper towels. Place a layer of sliced potatoes in dish; cover with onions. Sprinkle on some anchovies, garlic and rosemary. Season with salt and pepper and dot with part of remaining butter. Repeat until all potatoes and onions are used, finishing with a layer of potatoes.

Pour over milk and dot with remaining butter. Bake in oven about 40 minutes or until potatoes are cooked. Check occasionally and if browning too quickly, cover with foil.

Serve straight from dish, garnished with rosemary sprigs.

Makes 5 to 6 servings.

Note: These potatoes make a good accompaniment to grilled meats or they can be served for lunch with crusty bread and a crisp green salad.

ITALIAN MEATBALL HERO

1 tablespoon olive oil
1 small onion, finely chopped
1 garlic clove, crushed
2 teaspoons dried leaf oregano
1 (8 oz.) can tomatoes, drained, chopped
1 tablespoon tomato paste
1 French roll
2/3 lb. lean ground beef
Salt and pepper to taste
Vegetable oil for frying
1/3 cup butter, softened
6 oz. sliced mozzarella cheese
Sprigs of fresh watercress to garnish

To prepare tomato sauce, heat olive oil in a medium-size saucepan. Add onion, garlic, 1 teaspoon of oregano, tomatoes and tomato paste. Cook 10 minutes or until thick, stirring occasionally. Meanwhile, preheat oven to 375F (190C). Cut bread horizontally in half; do not cut through bottom crust. Remove all soft bread from center of both halves, leaving shell intact. Prepare 2 tablespoons of bread crumbs from soft bread. In a medium-size bowl, combine remaining bread crumbs and ground beef. Season with salt and pepper. Mix well. Form mixture in 12 small balls. Heat oil in a medium-size skillet. Add meatballs and fry 5 minutes or until set and golden. Drain on paper towels. Spread inside of bread shell with 2/3 of butter and add 1/2 of tomato sauce. Fill bread shell with meatballs and spoon sauce over meatballs. Cover with 1/2 of cheese slices. Press bread shell together. Spread outside of shell with remaining butter and cover with remaining slices of cheese and oregano. Wrap sandwich completely in greased foil. Bake in preheated oven 20 minutes. Unwrap foil to expose sandwich and bake 8 to 10 minutes more or until crisp. Cut in 4 thick pieces. Garnish with watercress.

Makes 4 pieces.

ITALIAN RICOTTA CREPES

7-inch crepes

1 cup ricotta cheese
1 tablespoon grated Parmesan cheese
1 tablespoon chopped fresh marjoram
Salt and pepper
2 tablespoons butter
2 tablespoons all-purpose flour
2 tablespoons tomato puree
2/3 cup chicken broth
Marjoram sprigs to garnish

Keep crepes warm while preparing filling. In a medium-size bowl, combine ricotta, Parmesan, marjoram, salt and pepper and beat until creamy. Divide filling between crepes. Fold in quarters and arrange in single layer in shallow heat-proof dish.

Preheat broiler. Melt butter in a small saucepan. Stir in flour. Cook, stirring, 30 seconds. Stir in tomato puree, broth, salt and pepper and simmer 3 minutes. Spoon over crepes. Broil until lightly browned, about 2 minutes. Garnish with sprigs of marjoram.

Serves 4.

MUSSELS WITH TOMATO SAUCE

12 fresh mussels
2 tablespoons butter
2 tomatoes, peeled, seeded, chopped
2 tablespoons chopped chives
2 tablespoons chopped fresh basil
1 clove garlic, crushed
1 tablespoon tomato paste
1/4 teaspoon salt
1/4 teaspoon ground black pepper
1/2 teaspoon sugar
6 slices brown bread
2 tablespoons vegetable oil
3 pitted prunes, cut in pieces, and basil leaves to
   garnish

Scrub mussels and remove beards. Place in a saucepan, cover and heat gently until shells have opened. Cool and discard any mussels that do not open. To prepare sauce, melt butter in a saucepan. Stir in tomatoes, chives, basil, garlic, tomato paste, salt, pepper and sugar. Bring to a boil, stirring occasionally. Cook gently 2 minutes or until thick.

Cut bread in 24 daisy shapes using a 1-inch daisy cutter. Heat oil in a skillet. Fry bread shapes until golden brown. Drain on paper towels. Remove mussels from shells; cut each in half and place on bread shapes. Top each with a spoonful of tomato filling and garnish with pieces of prune and basil leaves.

Makes 24 pieces.

LAMB & WALNUT BITES

8 oz. lamb fillet, cut up
1 cup soft bread crumbs
1 shallot
2 teaspoons fresh rosemary
1 teaspoon salt
1/2 teaspoon ground black pepper
1 egg
5 pickled walnuts
All-purpose flour
Rosemary sprigs to garnish

Sauce:
1 onion, finely chopped
1 clove garlic, crushed
3 large tomatoes, peeled, seeded, chopped
1 tablespoon chopped fresh basil
Oil for frying

In a food processor fitted with a metal blade, process lamb until finely chopped. Add bread crumbs, shallot, rosemary, salt, pepper and egg. Process until smooth. Cut pickled walnuts in small pieces. Using a little flour, press 1 teaspoonful of meat mixture in a flat round. Place a piece of walnut in center and form in a smooth ball. Repeat to make about 35 to 40 balls.

To prepare sauce, combine onion, garlic and tomatoes in a small saucepan. Bring to a boil and cook rapidly, stirring occasionally, until mixture is pulpy and thick. Stir in basil and pour into a serving dish. Half-fill a small pan with oil. Heat to 350F (175C) or to when a meat ball is placed in oil, it sizzles immediately. Fry meat balls in several batches 2 to 3 minutes or until lightly browned. Drain on paper towels. Serve with sauce. Garnish with rosemary sprigs.

Makes 35 to 40 pieces.

ITALIAN SPECIAL

1-1/2 teaspoons unsalted butter, softened
1 slice light or dark rye bread, cut
   diagonally in half
2 or 3 small red or green leaf lettuce leaves
2 slices prosciutto
2 or 3 slices mozzarella cheese
2 or 3 tomato slices
2 or 3 pitted black or green olives
1/2 teaspoon olive oil
1/2 teaspoon chopped fresh basil
Freshly ground pepper to taste
Sprigs of fresh basil to garnish

Butter bread. Cover buttered bread with lettuce leaves. Roll prosciutto in cone shaped rolls. Place rolls slightly to one side at a slight angle over lettuce leaves. Arrange an overlapping border of alternating cheese and tomato slices in front of rolls. Place olives in center of rolls. Drizzle olive oil over cheese and tomato slices, then sprinkle with chopped basil. Season with pepper. Garnish with sprigs of basil.

Makes 1 sandwich.

Variation: Substitute slices of salami, mortadella or bologna cut in half for prosciutto.

SALAMI SANDWICH

1-1/2 teaspoons unsalted butter, softened
1 slice light rye bread, cut diagonally in
   half
2 slices green peppercorn salami or
   pistachio Mortadella
3 or 4 radishes, sliced
1 tablespoon French dressing
4 pitted black olives
Gherkin pickle fan and sprigs of fresh
   cilantro to garnish

Butter bread. Cut slices of salami in half. Form each half in a cone shape. Place cones joined-side down on buttered bread, slightly overlapping. Dip radish slices into dressing. Arrange in overlapping rows over remaining area of buttered bread. Place an olive in each salami cone. Garnish with pickle fan and cilantro.

Makes 1 sandwich.

Note: To make a pickle fan, cut 3 or 4 (1/8-inch) slices from stalk end through to pointed ends of a small gherkin pickle. Carefully open slices to form a fan.

EGGS TAPENADE

6 hard-cooked eggs
18 ripe olives
5 flat anchovy fillets
1 tablespoon drained capers
1 (3-1/4 oz.) can tuna, drained
3 tablespoons olive oil
Lemon juice to taste
12 Italian parsley leaves

Shell eggs and cut each in half crosswise, using a silver or stainless steel knife (carbon steel leaves black marks on egg whites). Remove yolks and place in a food processor fitted with a metal blade. Trim bases of whites so eggs will sit flat. Set whites aside.

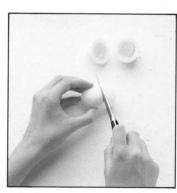

Remove pits from 12 olives, then place olives, anchovies, capers and drained tuna and egg yolks in food processor. Process until well blended. With motor running, gradually add oil to make a thick puree. Season with lemon juice. If preparing ahead, cover yolk mixture and refrigerate up to 2 days; place egg whites in a bowl, add cold water to cover and refrigerate up to 2 days. Drain whites, pat dry and fill just before serving.

To fill whites, spoon egg-yolk mixture into cavity of each one. Cut remaining 6 olives in half; place 1 half atop each filled egg half. Garnish with an Italian parsley leaf.

Makes 12.

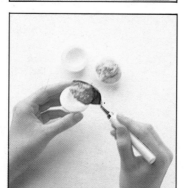

RICOTTA-CHEESE PUFFS

8 oz. ricotta cheese (1 cup)
2 eggs
2 tablespoons all-purpose flour
1 teaspoon salt
3 green onions, chopped
1/4 cup chopped parsley
2 teaspoons drained capers, coarsely chopped
Vegetable oil for deep-frying

Place cheese in a bowl and beat until smooth.

Beat in eggs, 1 at a time; then mix in flour, salt, green onions, parsley and capers. If preparing ahead, cover and refrigerate until ready to cook.

To cook, in a large heavy skillet, heat about 2 inches of oil to 350F (180C) or until a 1-inch bread cube turned golden brown in about 65 seconds. Drop rounded teaspoonfuls of ricotta mixture into hot oil, a few at a time. Cook until golden on all sides; drain on paper towels. Serve hot.

Makes about 20.

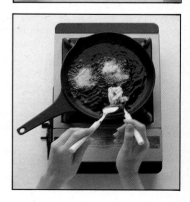

GORGONZOLA & NUT SHAPES — MOZZOLIVE BITES

1 recipe Traditional Pizza Dough, made up to end of step 2, page 40

Topping:
6 oz. Gorgonzola cheese
6 oz. mozzarella cheese
10 walnut halves
3 tablespoons walnut oil
Cucumber, to garnish

Preheat oven to 425F (220C). Grease a 14″ × 10″ jellyroll pan. Punch down dough and knead briefly. Roll out dough on a lightly floured surface and use to line bottom and sides of pan.

Cut cheeses into small cubes. Coarsely chop walnuts. Brush surface of dough with a little walnut oil. Sprinkle cheese over dough and top with walnuts. Drizzle with remaining oil.

Bake 20 minutes until dough is crisp and golden. Slide from pan onto a cutting board. Cut crusts off with a sharp knife and discard. Cut pizza into small squares and fingers. Garnish with cucumber and serve at once as a cocktail snack.

Makes 8 to 10 servings.

1 recipe Cornmeal Pizza Dough, made up to end of step 2, page 40

Topping:
4 tablespoons olive oil
6 oz. mozzarella cheese
1 (5-1/2 oz.) jar olive paste
Salt and pepper
Sage leaves and pimento, to garnish

Preheat oven to 425F (220C). Grease several baking sheets. Punch down dough and knead briefly. Roll out dough and cut into small circles or ovals. Brush with 1 tablespoon oil and bake 15 to 20 minutes until golden.

Cut cheese into tiny pieces and place in a medium bowl. Stir in the olive paste. Season to taste with salt and pepper. Spoon a little of the mixture onto each circle, dividing it equally among them.

Drizzle with remaining oil. Bake 3 to 4 minutes until cheese melts. Garnish with sage leaves and pimento. Serve at once as a cocktail snack.

Makes 10 to 12 servings.

DESSERTS

AMARETTI & ALMOND MOUSSE

FRAMBOISE ZABAGLIONE

1/2 cup whole blanched almonds
2 oz. amaretti cookies (macaroons)
3 eggs plus 2 egg yolks
1/3 cup superfine sugar
1 (1/4 oz.) envelope unflavored gelatin
    (1 tablespoon)
2 tablespoons lemon juice
1 to 2 tablespoons amaretto or kirsch
1-1/4 cups whipping cream

Toast nuts under broiler until brown. In a food processor fitted with the metal blade, process nuts and cookies to crumbs.

In a bowl, whisk eggs, extra yolks and sugar until thick and mousse-like. In a small bowl, sprinkle gelatin over lemon juice and let stand 2 to 3 minutes, until softened. Set bowl of gelatin in a saucepan of hot water and stir until dissolved. Reserve 1/4 of crumbs. Add gelatin, amaretto or kirsch and remaining crumbs to egg mixture. Whip cream stiffly. Reserve 1/3 of whipped cream and fold remaining into egg mixture.

Pour creamy mixture into a 4-cup soufflé dish and chill until set. Just before serving, using a pastry bag fitted with a star nozzle, pipe rosettes of reserved whipping cream on mousses and sprinkle with reserved crumbs.

Makes 6 to 8 servings.

Note: Amaretto is a very sweet liqueur made from almonds. Using kirsch instead gives a subtler flavor and makes the dessert less sweet.

4 egg yolks
3/4 cup plus 2 tablespoons framboise liqueur
1 tablespoon plus 2 teaspoons superfine sugar
Fresh strawberries and leaves to garnish, if
    desired
Langue de chats cookies to serve

Combine egg yolks, liqueur and sugar in a double boiler or a bowl set over a pan of simmering water.

Whisk mixture over medium heat until very thick and mousse-like, about 20 minutes.

Pour mixture into serving dishes. Garnish with strawberries and leaves, if desired, and serve immediately with cookies.

Makes 4 servings.

Note: It is important to use a whisk for this recipe. An electric mixer increases the volume of the eggs too quickly so that they do not have a chance to cook. The mixture will then collapse when poured into the serving dishes.

WHITE & DARK CHOCOLATE TERRINE

White Chocolate Mousse:
9 oz. white chocolate
1/2 (1/4 oz.) envelope unflavoured gelatin
    (1-1/2 teaspoons)
5 tablespoons water
1 tablespoon light corn syrup
2 egg yolks
2/3 cup whipping cream
2/3 cup dairy sour cream

Dark Chocolate Mousse:
6 oz. semisweet chocolate
1/4 cup strong coffee
2/3 (1/4 oz.) envelope unflavoured gelatin
    (2 teaspoons)
3 tablespoons water
8 tablespoons butter, cubed
2 egg yolks
1-1/4 cups whipping cream

Whipped cream and grated semisweet chocolate
    to decorate, if desired

Line an 8″ × 4″ loaf pan with plastic wrap to overlap edges. To prepare white chocolate mousse, break white chocolate in small pieces and set aside. In a small bowl, sprinkle gelatin over 2 tablespoons of water and let stand 2 to 3 minutes, until softened. In a saucepan, combine remaining water and corn syrup and bring to boil. Remove from heat and stir in gelatin until dissolved. Add chocolate pieces and beat until chocolate is melted and mixture is smooth.

Beat in egg yolks, 1 at a time. In a bowl, whip whipping cream and sour cream lightly and fold into chocolate mixture. Pour into prepared loaf pan and refrigerate until set.

To prepare dark chocolate mousse, in top of a double boiler or bowl set over a pan of simmering water, melt chocolate with coffee. In a small bowl, sprinkle gelatin over water and let stand 2 to 3 minutes, until softened. Set bowl of gelatin in a saucepan of hot water and stir until dissolved. Stir gelatin and butter into chocolate mixture and beat until butter has melted and mixture is smooth. Cool, then beat in egg yolks. In a bowl, whip cream lightly and fold into chocolate mixture.

Pour dark chocolate mixture over set white chocolate mousse. Refrigerate until set, then cover with overlapping plastic wrap and refrigerate overnight.

To serve, unfold plastic wrap from top and turn out onto a serving dish. Carefully peel off plastic wrap. Decorate with whipped cream and grated chocolate, if desired, and cut in slices.

Makes 8 to 10 servings.

ORANGE SORBET

Shredded peel of 1 orange
1-1/2 cups water
1 cup sugar
2 cups orange juice (about 4 large oranges)
1 cup uncarbonated mineral water

To Garnish:
Orange slices, if desired
Mint leaves, if desired

In a medium saucepan, simmer peel with water and sugar 20 minutes; cool. Strain sugar syrup. Set candied peel aside.

In a medium bowl, combine sugar syrup, orange juice and mineral water. Pour into ice cream canister. Freeze in ice cream maker according to manufacturer's directions. Fold in candied peel just before sorbet firmly freezes.

Freezer Method: Pour prepared mixture into several undivided ice trays. Place in freezer; freeze to a slush.

In a food processor/blender, process semi-frozen sorbet until smooth. Stir in orange peel. Return to trays; cover; freeze until firm.

Garnish with orange slices and mint leaves, if desired.

Makes 6 servings.

FIG & WALNUT CHEESECAKE

Filling:
3/4 cup dried figs, stems removed
Water
1 lb. ricotta cheese
2/3 cup whipping cream
2 eggs
2 tablespoons light-brown sugar
1 tablespoon all-purpose flour

Crust:
1/4 cup butter
1-1/4 cups graham cracker crumbs
1/2 cup ground walnuts

Garnish:
2 fresh figs
1 cup walnut halves

To prepare filling, cover figs with water in a saucepan. Bring to boil. Reduce heat, cover and simmer 15 minutes. Remove from heat and cool. Preheat oven to 325F (165C). Grease an 8-inch springform pan. To prepare crust, melt butter in a small saucepan over low heat. Stir in graham cracker crumbs and walnuts. Press mixture in greased pan. Set aside. Beat ricotta cheese, whipping cream, eggs and brown sugar in a large bowl until smooth. Coarsely chop figs. Stir figs and flour into cheese mixture. Spoon filling into prepared crust. Bake in preheated oven 1 hour and 10 minutes or until set. Cool before removing from pan. To garnish, trim tops from fresh figs; cut in slices. Arrange fig slices around edge of cheesecake. Place walnuts in center.

Makes 8 to 10 servings.

CHOCOLATE
ICE CREAM DECORATIONS

Chocolate goes beautifully with ice cream. Its crunch and strong flavor highlights ice cream's smooth texture and subtle flavors to perfection. Chocolate can be shaped into leaves, boxes or cups, curls and bations. Or, it can be used as a complete covering, either by being performed or poured over ice cream.

Chocolate Cups: Using a small brush, spread melted semisweet chocolate evenly over inside of foil baking cups. Cool. Refrigerate until firm. Before using, peel foil from chocolate.

Chocolate Leaves: Dip underside of leaves into melted semisweet or white chocolate. Or using a small brush, paint underside of leaves with melted chocolate. Place on a cookie sheet, chocolate-covered side upwards. Refrigerate until firm. Gently separate leaves from chocolate.

Other Decorations: Spread melted semisweet chocolate thinly on parchment paper. When chocolate begins to firm, cut out shapes to form into boxes or to use as tops for ice cream gâteaux, or shape into circles while chocolate is soft enough to mold. Let set. Carefully peel paper from chocolate.

Chocolate Curls: Chocolate block should be soft enough to scrape, but firm enough for the curls to hold their shape. Using a sharp vegetable peeler, peel off curls of chocolate. Use individually or roll curls together to make shapes. Larger rolls (chocolate batons) can be used as a garnish for parfaits.

Chocolate Caraque: Pour melted chocolate to a 1/8-inch thickness on back of cookie sheet. Let set. Holding cutting edge of a sharp knife at a 45 degree angle, push knife away from you, separating chocolate from cookie sheet. Chocolate will roll and form long scrolls as knife edge moves along under it.

SUGARED FRUIT, FLOWERS & LEAVES

Whole fruits with stems, flowers or leaves, rinsed, dried
1 egg white
Superfine sugar

In a small bowl, using a fork, lightly beat egg white until slightly frothy.

Holding by stem or inserting a fork into fruit, dip fruit, flowers or leaves in egg white. Or use a small brush to coat all surfaces evenly. Brush off excess.

Coat evenly with sugar. Dry on a sugared surface 30 minutes or until sugar forms a crisp, dry coating.

CHOCOLATE GELATO

3 cups milk
1 cup sugar
4 oz. semisweet chocolate, coarsely grated
Cookies, if desired

To Garnish:
Chocolate Caraque, page 83
Sugared Flowers, see left, if desired

In a medium saucepan, cook milk and sugar over low heat 10 minutes. Stir occasionally to dissolve sugar.

Mix chocolate with hot milk. Cook until chocolate completely dissolves.

Pour into ice cream canister. Cool. Freeze in ice cream maker according to manufacturer's directions. Cover.

Freezer Method: Pour prepared mixture into several ice trays, cool; cover. Place in freezer; freeze until firm. Using a fork, beat every 30 minutes 3 to 4 times while freezing.

Serve with a cookie, if desired.

Garnish with Chocolate Caraque and Sugared Flowers, if desired.

Makes 6 to 8 servings.

—PISTACHIO NUT ICE CREAM—

3 egg yolks
3/4 cup sugar
Vanilla extract to taste
2 cups light cream
Green food coloring, if desired
1 cup chopped pistachio nuts
Cookies, if desired

To Garnish:
Chopped pistachio nuts, if desired

In a stainless steel bowl or top of a double boiler, beat egg yolks, sugar and vanilla until thick and creamy.

In a small saucepan, scald 1/2 of cream. Add to eggs. Place bowl or top of double boiler over a pan of simmering water. Using a wooden spoon, stir slowly and continually until custard is thick enough to coat back of spoon. Remove from heat; cool. Pour custard, remaining cream, and food coloring, if desired, into ice cream canister. Freeze in ice cream maker according to manufacturer's directions. Fold in nuts just before ice cream firmly freezes.

Freezer Method: Stir remaining cream, nuts and food coloring, if desired, into custard. Pour prepared mixture into several undivided ice trays. Cover. Place in freezer. Freeze until firm, 3 to 6 hours. Using a fork, beat 2 times while freezing. Store in a covered container.

Serve with a cookie, if desired.

Garnish with chopped pistachio nuts, if desired.

Makes 6 servings.

NEAPOLITAN
—STRAWBERRY ICE CREAM—

3 cups fresh strawberries, pulped
1/2 cup sugar
1-1/2 cups whipping cream

To Garnish:
Fresh strawberries, if desired
Mint leaves, if desired

In a food processor/blender, process strawberries and sugar to smooth purée. Pour strawberry purée and cream into ice cream canister. Freeze in ice cream maker according to manufacturer's directions.

Freezer Method: In a medium bowl, lightly whip cream. Fold in strawberry purée. Pour mixture into several undivided trays. Cover. Place in freezer; freeze until firm, 3 to 6 hours. Using a fork, beat 2 to 3 times while freezing.

Store in a covered container.

Makes 6 to 8 servings.

CASSATA

Chocolate Gelato, page 84, softened
Vanilla Gelato, see right, softened
1 tablespoon chopped glacé cherries
1 tablespoon chopped candied peel
1 tablespoon chopped raisins
1 tablespoon chopped pistachio nuts
2 tablespoons Curaçao or other orange
   liqueur

To Garnish:
Maraschino cherries, if desired

Smoothly line a straight-sided loaf pan with foil.

Spread a 1/2-inch layer of Chocolate Gelato on sides, ends and bottom of pan, reserving enough to cover top. Freeze until hard.

In a medium bowl, mix Vanilla Gelato and remaining ingredients. Place in freezer.

When chocolate base is frozen, fill with Vanilla Gelato mixture. Cover lightly; freeze until firm. Cover top with remaining Chocolate Gelato; freeze again.
Serve sliced.
Garnish with cherries, if desired.

Makes 8 servings.

VANILLA GELATO

3 cups milk
1 vanilla bean
3/4 cup sugar

To Garnish:
Sugared Fruit, page 84, if desired
Mint leaves, if desired

In a saucepan, bring milk and vanilla bean to boiling point. Remove from heat; cool. When bean is soft, insert point of a small, sharp knife near top. Cut in 1/2. Scrape small seeds into milk. Stir in sugar until dissolved; cool.

Strain milk through a fine nylon strainer into ice cream canister. Freeze in ice cream maker according to manufacturer's directions.

Freezer Method: Strain milk into several undivided ice trays; cover; place in freezer; freeze until firm. Using a fork, beat every 30 minutes, during freezing.

Garnish with Sugared Fruit and mint leaves, if desired.

Makes 6 servings.

—COFFEE CHIFFON DESSERTS—

AMARETTI MERINGUE BOMBES

1/4 cup butter
3 tablespoons light corn syrup
2 cups vanilla wafer crumbs
2/3 cup whipping cream, whipped, and liqueur coffe beans to decorate

Filling:
3 tablespoons cornstarch
1/4 cup superfine sugar
1 tablespoon instant coffee granules
1-1/4 cups milk
2 eggs, separated
1 tablespoon plus 2 teaspoons plain gelatin
3 tablespoons hot water
1-1/4 cups whipping cream

In a saucepan, heat butter and corn syrup until melted. Stir in cookie crumbs and mix together evenly. Divide mixture among 8 plastic wrap-lined tiny molds and press mixture evenly over bottom and up sides of molds. Chill. To prepare filling, mix cornstarch, sugar, coffee and milk in a saucepan. Bring to a boil, stirring constantly, and cook 2 minutes. Remove from heat. Beat in egg yolks. In a small bowl, sprinkle gelatin over hot water; let stand to soften. Set bowl in a saucepan of hot water. Stir until dissolved and quite hot. Stir gelatin into coffee mixture and let stand until thick but not set.

In a small bowl, whisk egg whites until stiff. In a medium bowl, whip cream until thick. Fold egg whites and whipped cream evenly into coffee mixture. Divide mixture among molds, filling each to top. Cover and chill. To serve, invert molds onto serving plates; remove plastic wrap.

To decorate, place whipped cream in a pastry bag fitted with a star nozzle. Pipe around bottom of molds. Decorate with coffee beans.

Makes 8 servings.

1 tablespoon butter, melted
20 Amaretti cookies (macaroons), crushed finely
12 oz. raspberries, thawed if frozen
1 tablespoon plus 1 teaspoon powdered sugar
Additional raspberries and mint sprigs to decorate
Amaretti cookies (macaroons), if desired

Filling:
2 cups coarsely crushed meringues
2-1/2 cups whipping cream
1/4 cup Amaretti cookies (macaroons), broken in small pieces
1/4 cup maraschino cherries, chopped
1/4 cup chocolate morsels

Brush insides of 8 tiny molds with melted butter. Divide crushed cookies among molds and shake well to coat evenly. Chill.

To prepare filling, mix meringues, cookie pieces, cherries and chocolate in a bowl. Stir to mix well. In another bowl, whip cream to soft peaks. Add meringue mixture to whipped cream and fold in very gently until evenly mixed. Fill each mold with meringue mixture, pressing down to pack evenly. Cover and freeze until needed. In a food processor fitted with a metal blade, process raspberries and powdered sugar to a purée. Sieve raspberry purée into a bowl.

Just before serving, dip each mold into hand-hot water and invert onto serving plates. Decorate with raspberries and mint sprigs. Serve with raspberry purée and cookies, if desired.

Makes 8 servings.

—TUTTI FRUTTI CHEESECAKE—

12 oz. cream cheese, softened
1/4 cup sugar
2 eggs
1 tablespoon unflavored gelatin
2 tablespoons water
1/4 cup slivered almonds
2 tablespoons grated orange peel
2 tablespoons grated lemon peel
1/4 cup chopped raisins
3 tablespoons Grand Marnier or orange
   liqueur
1/4 cup chopped glacé cherries
28 to 30 ladyfinger cookies

Garnish:
5 glacé cherries, cut in half
Angelica pieces, cut in strips

Grease an 8″ × 4″ loaf pan. To prepare filling, beat cream cheese, sugar and eggs in a large bowl until smooth. Combine gelatin and water in a small saucepan. Simmer until gelatin is completely dissolved; stir into cheese mixture. Stir in almonds, orange and lemon peels, raisins, Grand Marnier or orange liqueur and cherries. Spoon filling into greased pan. Cut ladyfingers to fit into pan; arrange on filling. Refrigerate 2 to 3 hours or until set. Turn cheesecake out onto a serving dish. Garnish with cherry halves and angelica strips.

Makes 10 servings.

——CAMPARI CHEESECAKE——

Crust:
1/3 cup butter
1-3/4 cups graham cracker crumbs

Filling:
8 oz. Neufchâtel cheese, softened
2/3 cup plain yogurt
2/3 cup whipping cream
Finely grated peel and juice of 1 pink
   grapefruit
1/3 cup Campari
4 teaspoons unflavored gelatin
2 tablespoons water
2 eggs
1/4 cup sugar

Garnish:
2 pink grapefruit
2 kiwifruit
4 to 5 maraschino cherries, cut in half

Grease an 8-inch springform pan. To prepare crust, melt butter in a small saucepan over low heat. Stir in graham cracker crumbs. Press mixture in greased pan. Set aside. To prepare filling, beat Neufchâtel cheese, yogurt and whipping cream in a large bowl until smooth. Beat in grapefruit peel and juice and Campari. Combine gelatin and water in a small saucepan. Simmer until gelatin is completely dissolved; stir into cheese mixture. Beat eggs with sugar until they are thick and foamy and hold a ribbon when drawn across surface; fold into cheese mixture. Spoon filling into prepared crust. Refrigerate 2 to 3 hours or until set. Remove cheesecake from pan. To garnish, peel and cut grapfruit in segments. Peel and slice kiwifruit. Arrange grapefruit, kiwifruit and cherries around edge of cheesecake.

Makes 8 to 10 servings.

CANNOLI

Pastry:
1-1/2 cups all-purpose flour
2 tablespoons powdered sugar
2 tablespoons unsalted butter
2 tablespoons sweet sherry
2 tablespoons strong coffee
Vegetable oil for deep frying

Filling:
10 oz. mascarpone cheese
1/3 cup powdered sugar, sifted
1/4 cup chopped pistachios
1/3 cup chopped glacé fruits

To Decorate:
Sifted powdered sugar

To make pastry, sift flour and powdered sugar into a bowl. Cut in butter, then stir in sherry and coffee. Mix to a firm dough, knead lightly, cover and chill 30 minutes.

On a lightly floured surface, roll out pastry as thinly as possible. Cut out 14 (3-1/2-inch) squares. Lightly grease several cream-horn molds. Wrap a square of pastry around each mold, forming a cone. Moisten edges with water to seal.

Deep-fry 3 or 4 cannoli at a time on molds 1 to 2 minutes, until crisp and golden. Drain on paper towels. Remove from molds and let stand until completely cold.

To make filling, in a bowl, beat mascarpone, powdered sugar, nuts and glacé fruits. Use to fill cannoli. Dust with powdered sugar. Serve within 1 to 2 hours of filling.

Makes 14 cannoli.

Note: Cannoli are traditionally made on tube-shaped molds which are available in some kitchen stores. Lengths of 1-inch dowelling could be used as an alternative.

TIRAMI SU

Cake:
3 eggs
1/2 cup plus 1 tablespoon superfine sugar
3/4 cup all-purpose flour
1 tablespoon instant coffee granules, if desired

Filling:
12 oz. mascarpone cheese
4 egg yolks
1/2 cup superfine sugar
2 tablespoons rum
2 egg whites

To finish:
3/4 cup coffee
2 (1 oz.) squares semi-sweet chocolate, grated

To make cake, preheat oven to 350F (175C). Grease and line a deep 8-inch round cake pan with waxed paper.

In a bowl, whisk eggs and sugar until thick and light. Sift flour and coffee granules, if desired, over mixture, then fold in gently.

Spoon mixture into prepared pan and bake in oven 30 minutes, until golden and cake springs back when pressed in center. Turn onto a wire rack to cool.

To make filling, in a bowl, beat mascarpone until soft. In another bowl, whisk egg yolks and sugar until thick and light. Stir in mascarpone and rum. In a clean bowl, whisk egg whites until soft peaks form; fold into cheese mixture.

Cut cake horizontally in 3 layers. Put 1 layer on a serving plate. Sprinkle with 1/3 of coffee. Cover with 1/3 of filling. Repeat layers, finishing with a topping of cheese mixture. Chill overnight.

Sprinkle with grated chocolate to serve.

Make 8 servings.

AMARETTI CHEESECAKE

Crust:
1/4 cup butter
1/2 cup crushed vanilla wafers
1 cup soft macaroon pieces

Filling:
1 lb. Neufchâtel cheese, softened
2/3 cup sour cream
1/3 cup plus 3 tablespoons sugar
3 eggs, separated
1 tablespoon all-purpose flour
1/2 teaspoon almond extract
Finely grated peel and juice of 1 lemon

Garnish:
1 (16 oz.) can apricot halves, drained
2/3 cup whipping cream

Grease a 9-inch springform pan. To prepare crust, melt butter in a small saucepan over low heat. Stir in crushed vanilla wafers and macaroon pieces. Press mixture in bottom of greased pan. Set aside. To prepare filling, beat Neufchâtel cheese, sour cream and 1/3 cup sugar in a large bowl until smooth. Stir in egg yolks, flour, almond extract and lemon peel and juice. Beat egg whites with remaining sugar until soft peaks form; fold into cheese mixture. Spoon filling into prepared crust. Refrigerate 2 to 3 hours or until set. Remove from pan. To garnish, arrange apricot halves on cheesecake. Whip cream until stiff. Pipe (with a pastry bag) small whipped cream rosettes in between each apricot half and chill before serving.

Makes 12 servings.

FRUITS IN WINE

2/3 cup sweet white wine
2/3 cup sweet red wine
1-1/4 cups water
1/4 cup superfine sugar
4 strips lemon peel
2 teaspoons ground mace
6 fresh lemon balm leaves
6 ripe apricots
1/4 cup light-brown sugar
1 (2-inch) piece cinnamon stick
4 whole cloves
4 strips orange peel
6 fresh mint leaves
6 red plums
Fresh mint and lemon balm leaves and
    orange twists to decorate

Pour white and red wine into separate saucepans, each with 1/2 of water. Stir sugar, lemon peel, mace and lemon balm leaves into white wine. Bring to a boil. Add apricots, cover and simmer 5 to 8 minutes or until apricots are tender. Carefully spoon apricots into a small bowl. Cover with marinade so apricots are completely immersed. Refrigerate until cold. Meanwhile, stir brown sugar, cinnamon, cloves, orange peel and mint leaves into red wine. Bring to a boil. Add plums, cover and simmer 8 to 10 minutes until plums are tender. Carefully spoon plums into a small bowl. Cover with marinade so plums are completely immersed. Refrigerate until cold. Remove apricots and plums from syrup. Place on separate serving plates. Strain each marinade back into separate saucepans and boil rapidly 1 to 2 minutes or until syrupy. Pour red syrup over plums and white syrup over apricots. Refrigerate until cold. Decorate with mint and lemon leaves and orange twists.

Makes 3 servings.

LEMON MERINGUE PIZZA

1 recipe Traditional Pizza Dough, shaped
  and ready for topping, page 40

Topping:
3 tablespoons cornstarch
1-1/4 cups sugar
1/3 cup water
2 eggs, separated
Juice and grated peel of 2 lemons
Star fruit slices and lemon balm, to garnish

Preheat oven to 425F (220C). Prick
dough with a fork. Bake 20 minutes
until golden. Cool slightly. Reduce
oven temperature to 350F (175C).

Make topping. In a medium saucepan, combine cornstarch and 1 cup
sugar. In a small bowl, combine water
and egg yolk. Stir egg yolk mixture into
sugar mixture. Cook, stirring, over
medium heat until bubbly and thickened. Stir in lemon juice and peel. Spread
over baked crust.

In a large bowl, whisk egg white
until soft peaks form. Whisk in remaining sugar gradually. Pipe or spoon on
top of lemon mixture to cover filling
completely. Bake 10 minutes until
meringue is golden. Decorate with
slices of star fruit and lemon balm
leaves.

Makes 6 servings.

ALMOND RAVIOLI & RASPBERRY SAUCE

1-1/4 cups ground almonds
1/2 cup powdered sugar
2 egg yolks
2 tablespoons butter
1 recipe Fresh Pasta, see page 52
Plain yogurt
Raspberry leaves, if desired

Raspberry Sauce:
4 cups raspberries
1/2 cup powdered sugar

In a bowl, mix together ground
almonds, powdered sugar and egg
yolks. In a small saucepan, melt butter.
Add to almond mixture. Roll out pasta
dough, see page 52. Make ravioli, see
page 61, filling with ground almond
paste. In a large pan of boiling water,
cook ravioli about 10 minutes or until
tender but firm; drain. Make sauce.
Pour a pool of sauce on 4 dessert plates
and arrange ravioli on top. Spoon
yogurt into a pastry bag fitted with a
plain tip. Pipe a circle of yogurt around
each dish. Using a skewer, make a web
effect. Decorate with reserved raspberries and raspberry leaves, if desired.

Makes 4 servings.

To make sauce: Reserve a few raspberries for decoration. Mix remaining
raspberries and sugar in a medium-size
saucepan. Heat gently until juice
begins to run. Press through a sieve.

GRAPE BREAD

1 recipe Traditional Pizza Dough, made up
    to end of step 1, page 40
2 tablespoons fine sugar

Filling:
12 oz. red seedless grapes
1/4 cup fine sugar

To Serve:
Sugar and whipped cream

Preheat oven to 425F (220C). Grease a
deep 10-inch pizza pan or cake pan.

Spread grapes on a baking sheet and
bake 10 minutes. Meanwhile, punch
down dough and knead with 2 tablespoons sugar. Divide into 2 equal
pieces. Roll each piece to a 10-inch
circle. Remove grapes from oven; turn
off oven.

Place one dough circle in greased
pan. Brush surface with water and
spoon over half the grapes. Sprinkle
with half the remaining sugar. Lay
second piece of dough on top and press
gently with fingertips to seal dough
around grapes and make small pockets.

Spoon remaining grapes over the
surface and sprinkle with remaining
sugar. Cover with plastic wrap and let
rise in a warm place 1-1/2 hours. Preheat oven to 400F (205C). Bake 20 to
25 minutes until golden. Cool, then
dust with extra sugar and serve with
whipped cream.

Makes 6 servings.

CHRISTMAS CALZONE

1 recipe Traditional Pizza Dough, made up
    to end of step 1, page 40

Filling:
1/2 cup unsalted butter, softened
3/4 cup powdered sugar, sifted
2/3 cup packed brown sugar
1 tablespoon milk
1 tablespoon brandy
6 tablespoons mincemeat
Powdered sugar for dusting

Preheat oven to 425F (220C). Grease 2
baking sheets. Divide dough into
2 equal pieces. Roll out each piece to a
10-inch circle.

Make the filling. In a bowl, beat
butter and sugars together. Gradually
stir in milk and brandy until mixture is
light and fluffy.

Place 1 tablespoon brandy butter
and 3 tablespoons mincemeat to one
side of each circle of dough. Brush
edges with water, fold over and seal
edges firmly. Transfer to baking sheets
and bake 20 minutes until golden.

Dust with powdered sugar. Serve
warm with remaining brandy butter.

Makes 4 to 6 servings.

—FIG & PORT ICE CREAM—

1/2 cup superfine sugar
2/3 cup ruby port
1 (2-inch) piece cinnamon stick
6 fresh figs
1 tablespoon plus 1 teaspoon fresh lime
    juice
1-1/4 cups whipping cream
Crisp ice cream cups, if desired
Fresh fig slices and fresh mint leaves to
    decorate

In a medium-size saucepan, combine sugar and port. Simmer, stirring occasionally, until sugar has melted. Bring to a boil and add cinnamon and 6 figs. Cover and simmer 5 minutes. Let stand until completely cold. In a food processor fitted with a metal blade, process figs and liquid until smooth. Pour mixture into a sieve set over a bowl. Press mixture through sieve using a wooden spoon. Stir in lime juice. In a small bowl, whip cream until thick. Fold into fig puree until evenly blended. Pour mixture into a container. Cover and freeze 1 to 2 hours or until mixture is almost frozen but still soft. Return mixture to food processor. Process until thick and smooth. Return to container and freeze until firm. If desired, serve in crisp ice cream cups. Decorate with fig slices and mint.

Makes 6 servings.

—CHESTNUT & COFFEE BOMBE—

Chestnut Ice Cream:
3 eggs, separated
1/3 cup superfine sugar
1/2 cup unsweetened chestnut puree
2 tablespoons brandy
1-1/4 cups whipping cream

Coffee Sorbet:
1/4 cup superfine sugar
1-1/4 cups water
3 tablespoons finely ground coffee
1/2 egg white

To Decorate:
Chocolate leaves

To make chestnut ice cream, in a bowl, whisk egg yolks and superfine sugar until thick and light. In another bowl, mix chestnut puree and brandy until smooth.

In a third bowl, whip cream until just holding its shape. Fold chestnut puree into egg yolk mixture, then fold in whipped cream. In a clean bowl, whisk egg whites until soft peaks form; fold into mixture.

Pour mixture into a freezerproof container and freeze 1-1/2 to 2 hours, until nearly firm, stirring twice. Turn into a chilled 5-cup bombe mold or bowl and press around bottom and side. Return to freezer.

To make coffee sorbet, put sugar and water into a saucepan and heat gently, stirring constantly, until sugar has dissolved. Bring to a boil and boil 4 minutes. Stir in ground coffee, remove from heat and let stand 10 minutes to infuse. Pour through a fine sieve into a freezerproof container. Cool, then freeze 1 to 1-1/2 hours, until slushy. Transfer to a bowl.

In a bowl, beat egg white until soft peaks form; beat into coffee mixture. Pour into center of bombe mold and freeze about 2 hours, until firm.

Transfer to refrigerator 30 minutes before serving to soften. Turn out onto a serving plate and decorate with chocolate leaves.

Makes 8 servings.

—— FRUIT CHEESE DESSERT ——

1/4 cup Marsala wine
1/4 teaspoon ground mace
1 cup mixed glacé fruits, chopped
1-1/2 cups riccotta cheese or cream cheese
1 tablespoon plus 1 teaspoon superfine sugar
2 eggs, separated
2 teaspoons grated lemon peel
2/3 cup whipping cream
Fresh or glacé fruit and fresh mint sprigs to decorate

In a small bowl, combine wine, mace and glace fruits until well blended. Cover and let stand several hours. In a medium-size bowl, beat riccotta cheese, sugar, egg yolks and lemon peel with a wooden spoon until smooth. Stir in marinated fruit until well mixed. Whisk egg whites. Whip cream in a small bowl until soft peaks form. Using a spatula or metal spoon, alternately fold egg whites and whipped cream into cheese and fruit mixture. Spoon mixture into 6 small dessert dishes. Refrigerate 1 hour before serving. Decorate top of each dessert with fruit and mint sprigs.

Makes 6 servings.

LEMON GRANITA

Unlike sorbets which have a smooth soft texture, granitas are frozen flavored ices.

1 cup lemon juice (4 to 6 lemons)
2 cups water
1/2 cup sugar

To Garnish:
Mint leaves, if desired

In a medium bowl, mix juice, water and sugar. Stir until sugar completely dissolves. Pour into several undivided ice trays. Cover with foil. Place in freezer; freeze until firm.

Before serving, refrigerate to soften enough to scrape into dishes.

Garnish with mint leaves, if desired.

Makes 6 servings.

CHAMPAGNE & MINT GRANITA

3/4 cup superfine sugar
Pared peel and juice of 1 lemon
2 large bunches mint
1-3/4 cups water
1-3/4 cups champagne-type sparkling
  wine
Lemon slices and sprigs of mint to garnish

In a medium-size saucepan, combine sugar, lemon peel and juice, 1 bunch of mint and water. Heat gently, stirring constantly, until sugar dissolves. Bring to a boil and boil rapidly 5 minutes. Strain into a large bowl and add remaining mint. Cool. Remove mint and stir champagne into syrup. Pour into a shallow freezer container and freeze until slushy. Remove from freezer and beat or whisk until smooth. Repeat this process again, then freeze until set. Place granita in refrigerator 20 minutes before serving to make it easier to scoop. Spoon granita into frosted champagne glasses and garnish with lemon slices and sprigs of mint.

Makes 6 servings.

—ZABAGLIONE BAKED APPLES—

4 large baking apples
1/2 cup sliced almonds
1/3 cup dark raisins
1/2 cup dried apricots, chopped
Grated peel and juice of 1 lemon
1 tablespoon plus 1 teaspoon butter

Zabaglione:
2 egg yolks
2 tablespoons honey
2 tablespoons plus 2 teaspoons Marsala
  wine

Preheat oven to 350F (175C). Wash apples and core. In a small bowl, mix almonds, raisins, apricots and lemon peel. Make a shallow cut in skin around middle of each apple. Place apples in an ovenproof dish. Fill cavities with fruit mixture and pour lemon juice over fruit mixture. Top each apple with 1 teaspoon of butter. Bake in preheated oven 35 minutes. To prepare zabaglione, combine egg yolks, honey and wine in top of a double boiler or a bowl set over a pan of simmering water. Whisk constantly 7 to 10 minutes, until thick and fluffy. To serve, top apples with spoonfuls of zabaglione.

Makes 4 servings.

INDEX